Alcohol

DRUGS The Straight Facts

Alcohol

Cocaine

Hallucinogens

Heroin

Marijuana

Nicotine

■ **DRUGS**
The Straight Facts

Alcohol

Heather Lehr Wagner

Consulting Editor
David J. Triggle
University Professor
School of Pharmacy and Pharmaceutical Sciences
State University of New York at Buffalo

CHELSEA HOUSE
P U B L I S H E R S
A Haights Cross Communications ◆ Company
Philadelphia

CHELSEA HOUSE PUBLISHERS

VP, New Product Development Sally Cheney
Director of Production Kim Shinners
Creative Manager Takeshi Takahashi
Manufacturing Manager Diann Grasse

Staff for ALCOHOL

Associate Editor Bill Conn
Production Editor Jaimie Winkler
Picture Researcher Sarah Bloom
Series & Cover Designer Terry Mallon
Layout 21st Century Publishing and Communications, Inc.

A Haights Cross Communications ✦ Company

http://www.chelseahouse.com

First Printing

1 3 5 7 9 8 6 4 2

Library of Congress Cataloging-in-Publication Data

Wagner, Heather Lehr.
    Alcohol / by Heather Lehr Wagner.
        p. cm.—(Drugs, the straight facts)
Includes index.
    ISBN 0-7910-7260-6
    1. Alcohol—Juvenile literature. 2. Alcoholism—Juvenile literature. 3. Drinking
of alcoholic beverages—Juvenile literature. 4. Teenagers—Alcohol use—
Juvenile literature. [1. Alcohol. 2. Alcoholism.] I. Title. II. Series.
HV5066 .W34 2002
613.81—dc21

                                                                2002015919

Table of Contents

The Use and Abuse of Drugs

The issues associated with drug use and abuse in contemporary society are vexing subjects, fraught with political agendas and ideals that often obscure essential information that teens need to know to have intelligent discussions about how to best deal with the problems associated with drug use and abuse. *Drugs: The Straight Facts* aims to provide this essential information through straightforward explanations of how an individual drug or group of drugs works in both therapeutic and non-therapeutic conditions; with historical information about the use and abuse of specific drugs; with discussion of drug policies in the United States; and with an ample list of further reading.

From the start, the series uses the word *"drug"* to describe psychoactive substances that are used for medicinal or non-medicinal purposes. Included in this broad category are substances that are legal or illegal. It is worth noting that humans have used many of these substances for hundreds, if not thousands of years. For example, traces of marijuana and cocaine have been found in Egyptian mummies; the use of peyote and Amanita fungi has long been a component of religious ceremonies worldwide; and alcohol production and consumption have been an integral part of many human cultures' social and religious ceremonies. One can speculate about why early human societies chose to use such drugs. Perhaps, anything that could provide relief from the harshness of life—anything that could make the poor conditions and fatigue associated with hard work easier to bear—was considered a welcome tonic. Life was likely to be, according to the seventeenth century English philosopher Thomas Hobbes, *"poor, nasty, brutish and short."* One can also speculate about modern human societies' continued use and abuse of drugs. Whatever the reasons, the consequences of sustained drug use are not insignificant—addiction, overdose, incarceration, and drug wars—and must be dealt with by an informed citizenry.

The problem that faces our society today is how to break

the connection between our demand for drugs and the willingness of largely outside countries to supply this highly profitable trade. This is the same problem we have faced since narcotics and cocaine were outlawed by the Harrison Narcotic Act of 1914, and we have yet to defeat it despite current expenditures of approximately $20 billion per year on "the war on drugs." The first step in meeting any challenge is always an intelligent and informed citizenry. The purpose of this series is to educate our readers so that they can make informed decisions about issues related to drugs and drug abuse.

SUGGESTED ADDITIONAL READING

David T. Courtwright, *Forces of Habit. Drugs and the making of the modern world.* Cambridge, Mass.: Harvard University Press, 2001. David Courtwright is Professor of History at the University of North Florida.

Richard Davenport-Hines, *The Pursuit of Oblivion. A global history of narcotics.* New York: Norton, 2002. The author is a professional historian and a member of the Royal Historical Society.

Aldous Huxley, *Brave New World.* New York: Harper & Row, 1932. Huxley's book, written in 1932, paints a picture of a cloned society devoted to the pursuit only of happiness.

David J. Triggle
University Professor
School of Pharmacy and Pharmaceutical Sciences
State University of New York at Buffalo

1

Thinking about Drinking

Alcohol surrounds us. It is so much a part of our daily lives that we may not even notice how frequently we are exposed to it directly or indirectly. Beer commercials interrupt our favorite television programs; advertisements for wine pop up in the magazines we read. Billboards promoting a particular brand of liquor are plastered around our sports stadiums. In some states, beer and wine are sold in grocery stores and 24-hour convenience markets next to snacks and soft drinks.

Alcohol plays an important role in many celebrations. Champagne is used to toast a bride and groom at their wedding. Family parties may feature beer and wine. New Year's Eve parties offer the opportunity to mark the end of one year and the beginning of another with a drink in your hand.

Alcohol also has a significance in many ceremonies. In some religions, wine plays a symbolic role in certain sacred holidays and celebrations. In some cultures, wine and beer are regularly consumed as part of the family meal and a dinner is considered incomplete without this important element.

With all of these different customs and functions, alcohol presents a complex picture. It is important to remember that alcohol is a drug—a drug that can prove addictive and that alters the way your brain functions.

Alcohol plays an important and positive role in many celebrations and ceremonies. Alcohol is also a drug that affects the brain and body. Understanding and weighing the costs and benefits of alcohol use are essential for anyone thinking about drinking.

WHAT IS ALCOHOL?

Alcohol is defined as a colorless liquid obtained either synthetically or naturally, through the fermentation of certain carbohydrates (that is, transformation of carbohydrates to alcohol by means of enzyme activity). The colorless liquid

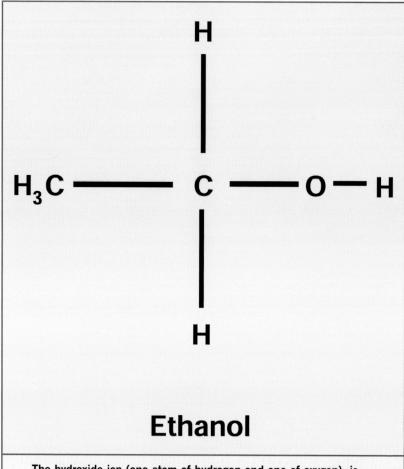

Ethanol

The hydroxide ion (one atom of hydrogen and one of oxygen), is the defining characteristic of an alcohol. The alcohol in alcoholic beverages like beer and wine is ethanol (C_2H_5OH).

we often describe as "alcohol"—the one that is used in beer, wine, and other alcoholic beverages—is known as ethyl alcohol or ethanol. It is created when yeast spores cause sugars to ferment.

Alcohol is most often created when fruits, grains, or vegetables are fermented. Yeast or bacteria affect the sugars in the grain, fruit, or vegetable, causing them to change chemically into alcohol. But alcohol can take different forms and is not only used for beverages.

Methanol, also known as methyl alcohol or wood alcohol, is an alcohol that offers several commercial uses. In earlier days, methanol was produced from wood, but it is now primarily created from methane, a component of natural gas. Methanol can be converted to formaldehyde and then used to make plastics. It also has uses as an industrial solvent in the manufacture of varnishes and paints and can be used as antifreeze and even as an alternative to traditional forms of automobile fuel.

Propanol, also known as propyl alcohol, is made from ethylene and a mixture of carbon monoxide and hydrogen. Its commercial applications include serving as a solvent for resins, and in the form known as isopropanol it can be found in rubbing alcohol as well as in certain cosmetics.

Ethanediol is yet another form of alcohol. Also known as ethylene glycol, it can be used as antifreeze in car radiators.

There are many forms of alcohol—some more toxic than others, some created from more complicated processes, and some with very specific commercial applications. There are even so-called "detergent alcohols," whose ability to dissolve dirt has made them useful in detergents, soaps, and shampoos. For this book, we will focus on alcohol in its form as ethanol and its uses and abuses as a beverage.

ALCOHOL CONTENT

The amount of alcohol a drink contains depends on many factors: the type of yeast used, the amount and type of sugar used, and the temperature during the process of fermentation. Different combinations produce different beverages, which contain different concentrations of alcohol. Of the three basic types of alcoholic drinks—beer, wine, and liquor—each has a different alcohol content.

In general, beer brewed in America contains 3 to 6 percent

During the fermentation process, yeast converts the sugar from grapes (in wine production) or from grains (in beer production) into alcohol. In the production of other alcoholic drinks like whiskey, the alcohol is concentrated through a process known as distillation.

alcohol. The basic American beer is made from malted barley and hops (ripened and dried cones from the hop plant). Brewers mix the malted barley with water and grains such as corn or rice. When this mixture is heated, starches in the grains convert into sugar and other carbohydrates. Brewers then remove the grains and boil the mixture with hops for flavor. Yeast is then added to start the fermentation process, changing the sugar into alcohol. Brewers generally age the beer for several weeks or months to improve its flavor.

The process of fermenting grapes and berries produces wine. Wine can be made from other fruits as well, including apples and pears. Wine may even be made from certain plants, such as dandelions. Winemakers affect the flavor of the wine by choosing certain grapes or fruits to use and deciding when to harvest them. Grapes or berries are removed from their stems and crushed. For white wine, the skins and pulp are separated from the juice; for red wine, the skins and seeds are fermented along with the juice. Yeast then converts the sugar in the grapes or fruit into alcohol.

Temperature affects the rate at which fermentation takes place. Red wines are generally fermented at a higher temperature for a shorter period of time than that for white wines. The wine is then aged in barrels or stainless-steel tanks. Wine varies in its alcohol content, generally containing about 10 percent alcohol. Some wines, including sherry and port wines, are described as "fortified" to indicate that ethanol has been added. These wines have an even higher alcohol content.

Alcoholic beverages other than wine may contain a higher alcohol content than wine. Whiskey, for example, is made from grain (generally corn), which then undergoes a distillation process to increase the amount of alcohol it contains. The fermented mixture of grain (sometimes called mash) is heated in a closed container. The ethanol boils up as steam. It then is separated, cooled, and re-liquefied.

Alcoholic beverages containing this type of purer ethyl alcohol are generally described as distilled. Their alcoholic content ranges from 40 to 50 percent.

How can you tell how much alcohol a drink contains? Some beers and wines list the alcohol content directly on their label. Other types of alcoholic beverages use the word "proof" on their labels. To find out the alcoholic content of these beverages, divide the proof in half. For example, a vodka or whiskey that claims to be "80 proof" contains 40 percent alcohol.

Even though alcoholic beverages contain different amounts of alcohol, this does not mean that one is more dangerous or addictive than another. Distilled spirits are not somehow "worse" than beer or wine. You can become addicted to alcohol no matter how it is packaged.

HOW DOES ALCOHOL AFFECT YOU?

Many people drink because alcohol makes them feel relaxed or happy. But alcohol is not a stimulant. It is a depressant, and it has a depressant effect on the brain's functioning. Consumption of alcohol can injure brain tissue and interfere with the parts of the brain that control memories, emotions, and thinking.

Your nervous system consists of a mixture of signals — some that excite or stimulate responses, and others that inhibit responses. Many of these signals happen without your awareness. But alcohol affects this complex balance of signals. Because alcohol is a depressant, it depresses specific parts of the brain, including those mechanisms that would normally inhibit certain responses. This is why alcohol can create the false impression of being a stimulant. But it is important to remember that alcohol is not stimulating a certain response — making you feel more outgoing or affectionate, for example. Instead, it is depressing certain parts of your brain that would normally inhibit those responses. It prevents them from their performing their normal functions.

When we think about alcohol's effects, we often think about what comes after too much alcohol—things like headaches, nausea, and a hangover the next day. But there are serious and specific ways in which alcohol affects the body as it is consumed, traveling from the stomach to the small intestine into the bloodstream and on to the brain, heart, and liver. Alcohol can damage different organs in the body and has been linked to heart disease, cancer, and the development of mental retardation and physical problems in newborns whose mothers drank while pregnant.

Alcohol affects your body, even in small doses. Small amounts cause your stomach to secrete gastric juices. Small

Josh likes to spike his orange juice with alcohol before he leaves for school in the morning. He isn't too picky about what he mixes in it. He just takes one of the bottles his father keeps in the kitchen cabinet, pours a little into a glass, and then adds some juice. Josh feels lonely at home and bored at school. If he has something to drink, those feelings slip away. He likes the relaxed, mellow feeling it gives him. When he comes home from school, he drinks more—either more alcohol mixed in a glass of Coke or a beer from the cans kept in the refrigerator.

Josh's dad doesn't notice his drinking. He leaves for work before Josh wakes up and isn't home until late in the evening. Josh carefully refills the bottles with water and crushes any beer cans into flat pancakes, then buries them deep in the garbage can.

Josh may not have the straight facts about the acute and chronic health effects that his pattern of alcohol use is inviting.

amounts cause your heart to beat faster and your blood pressure to rise. Alcohol causes the blood vessels within your muscles to constrict and those at the surface to expand, causing your skin to rapidly lose heat. This is what makes your skin appear redder or more flushed after you have had something to drink.

Alcohol affects your endocrine system—the glands that produce hormones. It causes you to urinate more, possibly causing dehydration. It stops the release of the hormone ADH (anti-diuretic hormone), the hormone that controls how much water the kidneys reabsorb and how much they excrete.

Alcohol affects various parts of the brain. One or two drinks affect the surface of the brain, whereas more can impair reasoning, control, and even the medulla's ability to regulate such involuntary responses as your heartbeat and your breathing. More drinks affect the cerebellum, impairing your ability to keep your balance.

Alcohol travels rapidly through your body, affecting— and impairing—its operation in many ways.

THE DANGERS OF DRINKING

Because alcohol impairs your brain's ability to function, drinking alcohol can be especially dangerous when the drinker then gets behind the wheel of an automobile. The leading cause of death for teenagers is automobile accidents, and some estimates suggest that alcohol is a factor in nearly half of these crashes.

Alcohol also poses other dangers for teens. Its depressant effect can prompt some to consider suicide. Alcohol consumption can be a factor in sexual assaults and date rapes. It can contribute to violent behavior and is often a factor in homicides and fatal injuries. In short, alcohol can create side effects that are not merely dangerous for the drinker, but for others around him or her. Teens need to be aware of what

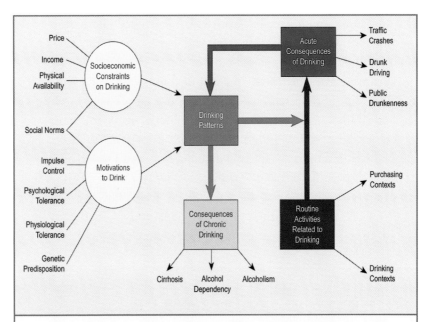

This schematic diagram highlights the interactions between influences, motivating factors, drinking patterns, and routine activities and consequences related to using alcohol. The complex relationship between acceptable alcohol use and the development of alcoholism is different for every drinker and is influenced by the individual's environment, body chemistry, and genetic predisposition.

alcohol is and how it affects their bodies before they decide to take that drink.

MAKING WISE CHOICES

Even though alcohol is a widely available beverage, legally sold and consumed by anyone over the age of 21, it is still a drug. It is a drug that can affect the way your body works now and how well it may function in the future. It can be addictive, and its abuse can prove dangerous both for the drinker and for others.

In later chapters, you will read about teens making

decisions about alcohol. You will learn more about how alcohol affects the body. You will learn about the legal issues surrounding alcohol and how these laws have changed over the years. You will find out some surprising statistics about alcohol and learn more about the people most likely to use and abuse it. Finally, you will learn about how to deal with alcohol addiction—how to prevent problems, how to ask for help if you need it, and what to do if you suspect that a friend or family member is abusing alcohol. This information will help you make wise choices when you are dealing with alcohol. Perhaps you have already been at a party where you were offered an alcoholic drink.

ALCOHOL AND TEENS: THE STRAIGHT FACTS

Alcohol is the oldest and most widely used drug in the world. But did you know these facts about alcohol?

- Nearly half of all Americans over the age of 12 are consumers of alcohol.
- There are an estimated 10 to 15 million problem drinkers or alcoholics in the United States.
- More than 100,000 deaths in the United States each year can be attributed to alcohol.
- As many as 4.5 million teens can be described as alcoholics or problem drinkers.
- Approximately half of all fatal automobile accidents in the United States are alcohol-related.
- There is no known "safe dose" of alcohol for teens—the ongoing process of development during adolescence means teens are more vulnerable to alcohol dependence and developmental disabilities than adults who drink.

[Source: American Council for Drug Education; PRIDE Surveys]

Maybe you have a friend or family member whom you suspect is an alcoholic. In the following chapters you will learn more about alcohol and begin to understand how it can affect you.

2

Alcohol:
Past and Present

No one knows precisely when the first alcoholic beverage was consumed, but one thing is certain: it was thousands of years ago. Many of the most ancient historical documents contain references to drinking. Records show that wine and beer were consumed in the Neolithic Age, and many ancient civilizations viewed these drinks as gifts from the gods. Certain cultures worshipped a god of wine— in ancient Rome the god was Bacchus; in ancient Greece he was called Dionysius; in ancient Egypt he was Osiris. Wine and beer played a role in these ancient civilizations, contributing both to rituals and celebrations. The Bible contains many references to wine. And other ancient texts also contain references to drunkenness and caution against drinking too much.

The word alcohol comes from an Arabic phrase, *al kohl*. Distilled spirits were first discovered in the tenth century by an Arabian doctor named Rhazes, who had been experimenting with a way to release what was described as "the spirit of the wine." The phrase *al kohl* referred originally to a finely ground powder used for eye makeup, but its meaning gradually expanded to refer to any kind of finely ground material. Soon it expanded further to define a revealed essence of something—including, in this case, the essence of wine.

Initially, distilled spirits were used for medical purposes—to cure fevers and colds, to provide pain relief, even to help children get to sleep. By the Middle Ages, the use of these distilled spirits

Bacchus was sculpted by Michelangelo in the 15th century. Some of the earliest references to alcohol use were recorded by the Egyptians in 3500 B.C., but many scholars believe the use of alcohol is as old as the human race itself.

had expanded from medicinal to more common, popular uses. Wine and beer played an important role in religious events, diplomatic occasions, and celebrations of all kind. They were also considered to be much safer to drink than water, whose contents and purity varied greatly from one source to another.

The earliest explorers to America brought alcohol with them. The colonists who arrived on the Mayflower agreed to come ashore at Plymouth, Massachusetts, in part because their provisions—including their beer—had all been used up in the journey across the Atlantic Ocean. Missionaries from Spain who came to the New World brought grapevines with them, making wine in the geographical area that would become California before the United States had gained its independence.

But with alcohol came trouble. By 1619, public drunkenness had been made illegal in the colony of Virginia, a crime punishable by whipping, fines, and even time in the stockade (prison).

THE TEMPERANCE MOVEMENT

Concerns about alcohol use and abuse grew in the 1800s with the spread of saloons in the new western frontier. A group of reformers banded together with the initial goal of promoting more moderate drinking. Their movement, known as the Temperance Movement (temperance meaning moderation or self-restraint), started as part of a wave of social reforms, including focuses on child labor, women's rights, and the abolition of slavery, and the initial call was for more moderate drinking to avoid excessive drunkenness. By the 1850s, however, the Temperance Movement had sparked the creation of several other groups, such as the Independent Order of Good Templars, the Women's Christian Temperance Union, and the Anti-Saloon League, all of which publicly proclaimed the evils of liquor. By 1869, many of these groups had banded together to form the National Prohibition Party, a political party that called for making alcohol illegal.

The Prohibition movement became a way for women to begin to exercise some political influence. At the time, women in the United States had no direct political power—they did not have the right to vote, let alone run for office themselves—and many women began to rally around the Prohibition movement as a way to begin to affect the political process. Their forms of protest involved things such as demonstrations, prayer vigils, encouraging people to sign petitions, and even public gatherings during which hymns were sung. The women's goal was to convince people of the evils of saloons and, ultimately, to persuade the people who ran and managed the saloons to destroy their liquor and close their businesses.

WOMAN'S CRUSADE

The efforts of women around the country ultimately resulted in the Woman's Crusade of 1873–74. One of the leaders of this movement was Eliza Daniel Stewart, a woman who was often referred to as "Mother Stewart." Stewart had worked in the Sanitary Commission (an early forerunner of the Red Cross) during the American Civil War. The experience provided her with a certain amount of leadership skills— skills that she later used during the Women's Crusade as one of its founders and, then as an international speaker on temperance issues. Stewart traveled to Britain, where she helped to form the British Woman's Temperance Association. Still later, she supported the formation of the Prohibition Party, sponsoring several politicians including a candidate for the U.S. presidency. She published her memoirs in a popularly acclaimed book of the time, *Memories of the Crusade, A Thrilling Account of the Great Uprising of the Women of Ohio in 1873, Against the Liquor Crime.*

The increase in calls for the prohibition (or banning) of the sales of alcohol coincided with the rapid expansion of the American brewing industry in the late 1800s. German immigrants had brought beer (and beer brewing) with them to the United States, and by 1890 beer had become the largest-selling alcoholic beverage in the country. Large American brewers, such as Pabst and Annheuser Busch, shipped their product west by railroad, expanding their markets nationwide by means of saloons. Brewers developed their own saloons, where only their own particular brand of beer was sold. Fierce competition broke out among the

Groups like the Women's Christian Temperance Movement of the late 19th century proclaimed the evils of alcohol use. These women marched on Washington, D.C. in 1909 to present a petition supporting Prohibition.

different brewers, as one saloon after another attempted to win customers.

In an effort to build business, saloons tried to attract customers by offering free lunches (heavily salted, to encourage customers to drink more) and tried to attract younger and younger men into their businesses. The saloon's "business" soon expanded to include gambling and even prostitution.

It is not surprising that many Americans came to view saloons—and the alcohol they sold—with distaste. The Prohibition Party was founded in 1869, created to offer candidates for office who were committed to the banning of alcohol. The party put forward candidates for local, state, and even national office in many parts of the United States, but the party itself suffered from internal divisions, with members split between wanting a party that focused solely on the issue of alcohol to a more broad-based party that offered positions on many national issues.

Nonetheless, the calls for reform grew. By 1919, the reform movements had succeeded in passing the 18th Amendment to the Constitution, making it illegal to manufacture, distribute, or sell alcoholic beverages.

PROHIBITION

The period from 1920 to 1933, when the 18th Amendment was in effect, is often referred to as Prohibition. During this period, there was only one legal way to obtain alcoholic beverages: with a doctor's prescription, alcohol could be bought at a pharmacy. Certain distilled spirits—generally brandy or whiskey—were felt to have medicinal purposes, and doctors could write out a prescription, using a special government form, for their use.

Prohibition succeeded in regulating the legal sale of alcoholic beverages, but it never succeeded in preventing people from drinking alcohol. The regulations designed to implement Prohibition were messy and confusing, with some 60 different provisions to the Volstead Act—the act designed to ensure that Prohibition was carried out. An underground industry of illegal venues for manufacturing and distributing alcohol soon grew. Many major American cities had "speakeasies"—private clubs where alcohol was quietly distributed. The period of Prohibition created a powerful new group of gangsters, who organized the manufacture and illegal sale of alcohol. This was the beginning of many of the organized crime "families," who continue to challenge law enforcement officials today.

The number of deaths attributed to cirrhosis (the disease of the liver caused by excessive alcohol consumption) declined during Prohibition; nonetheless, most experts view the period as a failure. The real problems that led to drunkenness were never fully addressed, and once the law was repealed in 1933 as the 21st Amendment to the Constitution, legal use of alcohol resumed.

The 21st Amendment shifted the power to control and regulate alcoholic beverages to the individual states. Each state now has its own separate bureaucracy for enforcing its own laws governing the consumption of alcoholic beverages. Rules vary greatly from state to state. In some states, beer and wine are sold in supermarkets and convenience stores. In others, only certain licensed businesses can sell alcohol. The strictest regulation occurs in certain states, such as Pennsylvania and Utah, which are known as "control states." In these states, alcoholic beverages are sold only in state-owned liquor stores.

The rise of Internet sales, as well as catalogues offering specialty wines and beers, has challenged this interpretation of the 21st Amendment and the individual state's ability to govern the distribution of alcoholic beverages. Some critics have expressed concern that underage drinkers might be able to purchase alcohol online. Debate continues regarding precisely what kind of regulation should govern this type of e-commerce. A few states have passed laws allowing their residents to "import" alcohol from other states, whereas the majority of states still find this action illegal.

RECENT HISTORY

Through the twentieth century, perspectives on the consumption of alcohol shifted as, gradually, medical research began to explore the dangers of alcohol. In 1956, the American Medical

People lined up and down Broadway in New York City to celebrate the repeal of the 18th Amendment and the end of Prohibition on April 7, 1933.

Association classified alcoholism as a disease and officially endorsed the policy of treating it as such. In 1970, Congress created the National Institute on Alcohol Abuse and Alcoholism to spark publicly funded alcohol research.

But the 1970s also brought a lowering of the legal drinking age to 18 in many states, when the legal voting age was also lowered to 18. The debate focused on the legal age of "maturity," with many arguing that if you were old enough to be drafted or to vote, then you also were old enough to drink alcoholic beverages.

A rise in deaths from traffic-related accidents soon followed the lowering of the legal drinking age. Large numbers of the victims were between the ages of 18 and 21, and many of these victims were determined to have been drinking when driving.

Groups such as Mothers Against Drunk Driving (MADD) and Students Against Drunk Driving (SADD)—known today as Students Against Destructive Decisions—were created to

DRUNK DRIVING: THE STRAIGHT FACTS

Alcohol is the oldest and most widely used drug in the world. But did you know these facts about alcohol?

- In 1997, alcohol-related crashes killed more than 16,000 people. That translates to one death every 32 minutes. And even more are injured due to alcohol-related accidents, an estimated one million people per year.

- The National Highway Traffic Safety Administration estimates that 3 out of every 10 Americans will be involved in a traffic accident related to alcohol at some time in their lives.

- It's not just the drinkers who are affected by alcohol. In 1996, 40 percent of the people who died in crashes involving drunk driving were *not* the drivers, but passengers in the car, people in another car struck by the drunk driver, or pedestrians.

- More than a million people are arrested each year for driving while intoxicated. More people are arrested for drunk driving than any other crime—nearly 10 percent of all arrests are for driving while intoxicated.

Source: 10th Special Report to the U.S. Congress on Alcohol and Health, U.S. Department of Health and Human Services, June 2000

respond to the threat posed by drinking and driving. The federal government was soon forced to respond to the public outcry. Pressure from these public service groups and the government forced states to change their drinking age. By 1988, all states had raised the minimum drinking age to 21.

The public service campaign soon spread to the beverages themselves. By 1989, all alcoholic beverages were required to carry warning labels detailing the health danger posed by consuming alcohol. Legal rulings found that bars and restaurants could be held responsible if a customer was allowed to drive after drinking too much.

ALCOHOL ADVERTISING

More recently, public interest groups such as MADD have focused on the alcohol industry's advertising campaigns, expressing concern that promotions for alcoholic beverages be restricted to avoid underage drinkers being exposed to these advertising campaigns. The debate was sparked by actions taken by the distilled spirits industry in November 1996, when the Distilled Spirits Council of the United States announced that it intended to change a policy that it had followed for 50 years—not to advertise its products on radio or television. The council justified its decision by arguing that the absence of advertising mistakenly gave the impression that its products were somehow "worse" than beer or wine and offered a commitment to ensure that its advertisements would target adults only.

The move drew a mixed response, with many (including then-president Bill Clinton) criticizing it as an irresponsible action. A subsequent study by the Federal Trade Commission (FTC) examined whether the alcoholic beverage industry was doing enough to make sure that its advertisements did not appeal to underage drinkers. One step was to recommend that advertisements for these products not be shown in movie theaters showing movies designed for a younger audience

Ad campaigns that use animated characters or animals to sell alcohol, like the Budweiser frogs, have been criticized by groups like Mothers Against Drunk Driving for encouraging children to drink. Budweiser pulled the successful ad because of the pressure.

(movies rated PG or PG-13, for example), on television programs with younger audiences, or on college campuses. The FTC did not go so far as to suggest that the government should step in to regulate the advertising of alcoholic beverages.

A five-year study is under way by the National Institute on Alcohol Abuse and Alcoholism and the Center for Substance Abuse Prevention, examining whether alcohol advertisements affect the drinking behavior of young people. The results are scheduled to be published in 2003.

DRUNK DRIVING

Because drinking can affect your balance and coordination, as well as your judgment and attention, it is especially dangerous to drink and drive or to get into a car with a driver who has been drinking. Recent actions by the government to penalize drunk drivers have contributed to a reduction in the number of motor vehicle accidents involving alcohol.

According to the National Highway Traffic Safety Administration (NHTSA), an accident is alcohol-related if either the driver or a pedestrian involved in the accident has a blood alcohol concentration (BAC) of 0.01 percent or more. But some states have taken a much more lenient approach, raising the BAC level to as high as 0.10 percent before describing someone as "legally intoxicated." (We will discuss BAC in greater detail in the next chapter.)

In 2000, President Bill Clinton signed legislation that required states to take a much stricter approach to drunk driving, lowering the BAC limit to 0.08 percent, or they will lose federal highway funding. Beginning in October 2003, states that have failed to pass this law will lose 2 percent of their highway funding and will continue to lose an additional 2 percent of the funding for each year that they fail to pass the law, up to a loss of 8 percent annually.

Studies support this stricter approach. In 2001, the NHTSA studied the role alcohol played in fatal automobile accidents in

Lowering the legal limit of blood alcohol concentration to 0.08% has resulted in a reduction of alcohol-related automobile fatalities for many states. Legislation passed in 2000 requires that all states adopt this standard by 2003 or risk losing funding for their highways.

states whose legal BAC limit was the lower 0.08 percent. The results showed that the number of alcohol-related accidents was declining. In 1987, alcohol-related accidents accounted for 51 percent of all fatal crashes; in 1999, the number had declined to 38 percent.

3

The Health Effects of Alcohol

Let's begin with an important fact: alcohol is a drug. Just like any drug, it has clear effects on your body, not only when you drink a lot, not only when you drink often. Each and every time you take a drink, the alcohol goes to work inside your body, changing the way your body functions.

Alcohol is a depressant. Although many people say that drinking makes them feel more stimulated and makes them experience more intense pleasure or feel more relaxed, these feelings are simply a result of alcohol depressing your brain.

Alcohol is absorbed quickly by your body. Unlike food, which requires the process of digestion to break it down and transform it in substances that the body needs, alcohol quickly passes into your bloodstream (through the capillaries in your mouth) and into your stomach. If there is food in your stomach, the alcohol will mix with it. This can help dilute the alcohol and slow its rate of absorption.

Again, alcohol passes into the bloodstream—up to 20 percent of it passing directly into the bloodstream from the stomach. What's left goes on to the pyloric valve. This valve acts as a kind of "gatekeeper," controlling what moves from the stomach into the small intestine. If large amounts of alcohol move through the body, the pyloric valve often stays shut, preventing it from moving into the small intestine. This action is a safeguard and prevents poisonous amounts of alcohol from passing into the small intestine. When this happens, the alcohol that is trapped in the stomach begins to prompt the

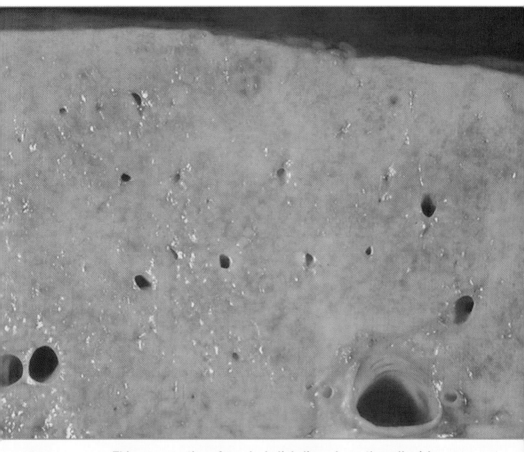

This cross-section of an alcoholic's liver shows the yellowish-orange color and scarring common to cirrhosis. Surveys estimate that cirrhosis of the liver is the seventh leading cause of death in the United States, and alcohol abuse is the most common cause of cirrhosis.

stomach lining to produce more and more hydrochloric acid—a digestive aid. But too much hydrochloric acid, mixed with too much alcohol, will make you feel nauseated and you may vomit.

When alcohol passes into the small intestine, it rapidly moves into the bloodstream, where it is carried throughout the body.

THE WEIGHT FACTOR

How quickly alcohol is absorbed by your body and how it affects you depends on the amount of alcohol you consume, but other factors matter as well. How much food you have in your stomach affects how quickly the alcohol is absorbed into your bloodstream. More food slows down the rate of absorption. And alcohol can race through your body if

Most of her friends were drinking at the graduation party, but Katie had said no. Now she felt as if she were in the middle of some sort of weird science experiment. Many of the kids around her were holding cans of beer. They were all drinking the same alcohol—some more, some less. But you could clearly tell who had been drinking—and not just from the way their breath smelled. The kids who had been drinking were talking louder and standing a lot closer to everybody else. They were laughing more, and their faces were red.

But it was strange that while the drinkers were the same in some ways, the beer seemed to be affecting them differently in other ways. For instance, Marcie seemed to be drunk already, even though she couldn't have had more than two beers. In fact, she was barely able to stand up. Tina seemed to be less inhibited. She was dancing around a group of boys and putting her arms around first one, then the other. Kevin was sitting quietly in a corner, drinking and looking depressed. And Carl, who had been drinking more than anyone else, didn't seem to be drunk at all. How was it possible that the same beer could affect her friends so differently?

What Katie may not have known is that alcohol affects different people in different ways, according to a variety of factors like the rate of alcohol absorption by the body, the drinker's weight, and the drinker's tolerance to alcohol's effects.

you take a drink on an empty stomach.

Your size and weight matter, too. Two 12-ounce cans of beer contain the same amount of alcohol, but one can of beer will give a higher blood alcohol level to someone who weighs 100 pounds than to someone who weighs 175 pounds. Why? It comes down to water—water that can dilute the alcohol. The smaller the body, the less water it contains and the less water is available to dilute the alcohol.

The amount of alcohol in your blood is usually called the blood alcohol concentration (BAC) or blood alcohol level (BAL). It measures the amount of alcohol (in milligrams, or mg) in 100 volumes (written in milliliters, or ml) of blood. BAC is often described in percentages and then abbreviated further, changing the milligrams to grams. So when a person's level of intoxication (or drunkenness) is described, you might see that a person with a BAC of 100 mg of alcohol per 100 ml of blood would be described as having a BAC of 0.10 percent.

At what point does it become difficult for your body to function? It depends on how much alcohol you consume, whether or not you had food in your stomach, how much you weigh, and also how quickly you drink the alcohol. The faster the alcohol races through your body, the more likely your body is to find it difficult to function normally.

Your body begins to discard the alcohol shortly after it is absorbed into the bloodstream—through urine, sweat, and even your breath. You can often smell alcohol on the breath of someone who has been drinking. This is why law enforcement officials often use Breathalyzers to measure whether or not a person has been drinking. A Breathalyzer measures the amount of alcohol in your exhaled breath. The amount you exhale is in proportion to the BAC in your body. So a Breathalyzer measures not simply how much you have had to drink but the more important factor—the blood alcohol level in your body.

A person who has consumed an alcoholic beverage exhales alcohol with each breath. The amount of alcohol exhaled is in proportion to the BAC, which is why Breathalyzers are able to measure an individual's level of intoxication.

JUST PASSING THROUGH

You discard some alcohol through urine, breath, and sweat, but this is only a small percentage (about 5 percent) of the alcohol your body has consumed. The rest continues to pass through your body as your body tries to metabolize (biochemically process) it in the same way that it metabolizes food into energy.

But alcohol does not work like a food. It is metabolized at a constant rate, unlike food, which can be metabolized faster with increased exercise or other calorie-burning activity. You cannot exercise more to get rid of the excess alcohol you consumed. You can't walk it off or run it off. You have to wait for it to be metabolized, generally up to two hours for a single glass of beer or wine.

Your body recognizes that alcohol is a foreign substance in the bloodstream and quickly sets to work to get rid of it. Enzymes in the liver act to metabolize the alcohol into acetic acid. The acetic acid then leaves the liver. In a chemical reaction, the acetic acid gradually travels through the body, being transformed by tissues and cells into carbon dioxide and water.

The liver's job is an important one. While different parts of the body help to oxidize the alcohol—to break it down into carbon dioxide and water—only the liver begins the process with its enzymes metabolizing the alcohol into acetic acid. For this reason, the liver is particularly sensitive to alcohol. Even small amounts of alcohol can spark the liver to begin to accumulate fat cells. In addition to metabolizing alcohol, the liver is critical to maintaining your correct blood sugar level. The liver stores this sugar (glucose) to ensure that the brain always has a ready supply of this critical energy to function. But when alcohol comes into the body, the liver gets distracted. It concentrates on metabolizing the alcohol. If you have not had enough to eat, the liver is faced with a problem—alcohol that needs to be metabolized plus no glucose to keep the brain cells functioning.

Your liver may then try to use protein and turn it into glucose, a process that the body can perform routinely with one exception—when alcohol is present. The alcohol acts to depress this process, preventing the liver from transforming stores of protein into glucose. What happens next? You do not have enough blood sugar in your body. Your brain does not have the glucose it needs to function. This is a condition known as hypoglycemia. You may feel a headache forming, or your body may feel shaky. You may feel weak, nervous, or hungry. You may begin to sweat. In severe cases, you may even slip into a coma.

You may think that the liver causes problems only for people who have been drinking for years. Think again. Studies have proved that if you have not been eating properly for a period of time as short as two days and then begin to drink heavily, you may experience the most severe symptoms of hypoglycemia.

EFFECTS ON YOUR BODY

As alcohol travels through your bloodstream, it affects the performance and functioning of different parts of the body. It affects your stomach by prompting it to produce gastric juices. But with too much alcohol, many of your body's functions are depressed, and that includes the stomach. Too much alcohol—and the process of digestion slows or even stops.

What about your heart and blood pressure? In small amounts, alcohol causes the blood vessels near the surface of the skin to expand. You may feel warm, and your skin may flush. But don't be fooled. Despite the feeling that you are getting warmer, alcohol is actually acting to cool off your body.

Next come the kidneys. Someone who has had several drinks may need to use the bathroom frequently. But something more is at work than simply the body's attempt to eliminate excess liquid. Alcohol affects the pituitary gland—a gland located at the base of the brain. The pituitary gland regulates many critical body functions, and one of these is the production of urine. The pituitary gland secretes a hormone that regulates urine production. Just as alcohol depresses the functioning of other parts of the body, it depresses the functioning of the pituitary gland, causing it to release too little of this critical hormone. The kidneys then respond by forming larger than normal amounts of diluted urine causing mild dehydration.

The brain is even more sensitive to the presence of alcohol—in fact, it is probably the part of the body most

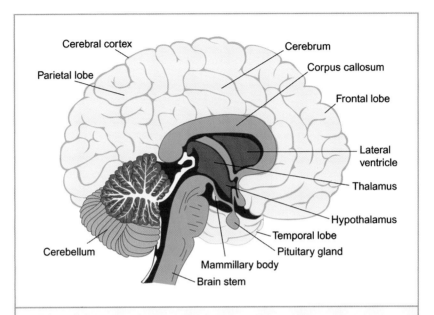

This cross section of the human brain shows the structures that are most affected by alcohol: the thalamus and hypothalamus (responsible for processing information from the sensory organs and regulating body temperature), the cerebral cortex and cerebellum (responsible for the coordination of sensory and motor information, coordination of muscles and equilibrium), and the pituitary gland (responsible for a hormone that regulates urine production).

strongly affected by alcohol. Alcohol has an impact on nerve cell membranes, the production and activity of neurotransmitters and receptors (controlling how the brain conveys messages from one nerve cell to another). It reduces a nerve's ability to send these messages, preventing it from properly processing information from the senses, the muscles, and even the skin. This prevents the brain from transmitting information critical for thinking and for bodily functions. In addition to blocking learning and memory, alcohol also blocks reasoning. People who have had too much to drink may still believe themselves fully capable of doing ordinary tasks—including driving.

THE DANGERS OF DRINKING AND DRIVING

Driving a car requires the body to perform tasks that are often described as "divided attention tasks." These are actions that require you to do more than one thing at once. When you are driving a car, you must maintain the car's speed, react to the twists and turns of the road, steer around obstacles, respond to signs and signals, and brake quickly if necessary. Each of these tasks on its own is fairly simple to do, but when combined they can turn into a more complex process, requiring you to pay attention to several different factors nearly simultaneously.

Alcohol affects your brain's ability to perform these divided attention tasks. The most basic tasks—stepping on the gas pedal, driving along a straight, familiar road—may still be possible, but your body will no longer be able to react quickly

TEENS DRIVING DRUNK: THE STRAIGHT FACTS

Alcohol affects your brain's ability to perform the complex assortment of tasks necessary to drive safely. And yet many teens ignore how alcohol may affect them when they get behind the wheel. Take a look at these statistics:

- Drivers aged 16–20 are three times as likely as older drivers to have had at least five drinks before driving.

- Drivers aged 16–20 are twice as likely as older drivers to drive less than an hour after drinking.

- Drivers aged 16–20 who drive after consuming alcohol have been found to have higher estimated blood alcohol concentrations—generally more than twice as high as those of older drivers.

Source: "Driving After Drug or Alcohol Use: Findings from the 1996 National Household Survey on Drug Abuse," Department of Health and Human Services and Department of Transportation.

to the unexpected. How would you react to a child suddenly stepping off the sidewalk in front of you, a car suddenly turning in front of you, a sharp curve in the road in front of you, flashing lights, or a loud noise?

And there's more. Alcohol can slow down the speed at which your body reacts. It can affect your ability to judge different sounds and different levels of light, as well as the speed and distance of moving objects. Your body becomes less coordinated. Your eyes adjust to changes in light more slowly, making night driving—and the glare of headlights from other cars—a particular danger.

Most dangerous of all, alcohol fools your brain. By impairing your judgment and reasoning, alcohol prevents your brain from recognizing that you've had too much to drink and shouldn't be driving. You will get behind the wheel believing that you have not had too much to drink and that you are fully capable of safely driving home. And many times, you will be wrong.

THE MORNING AFTER

While the body attempts to quickly metabolize the alcohol as soon as it enters the bloodstream, there is not much that can be done to speed up the passing of alcohol through the body. Depending on how much alcohol you have had to drink, how quickly you drank it, how much food was in your stomach, and how much you weigh, the process of becoming sober (when all alcohol has passed out of your body) takes time.

Many of the popular myths about "sobering someone up" are just that—myths. Drinking black coffee or taking a cold shower may make you feel more awake, but you will still have the same amount of alcohol in your system. And once your body has eliminated all of the alcohol from your system, you may then experience one of alcohol's most unpleasant side effects: a hangover.

A hangover is your body's final response to too much alcohol. There are many symptoms, and none of them is pleasant: headache, nausea, thirst, depression, anxiety, fatigue, irritability, dry mouth, and extreme sensitivity to sounds and light.

Why does your body react this way? In some cases, these are symptoms of dehydration (loss or reduction of fluids in the body). It seems ironic that drinking too much can cause you to become dehydrated, but it traces back to what we've learned about the functioning of the kidneys. When alcohol triggers the kidneys to produce increasing amounts of urine, more fluid is carried out of the body, causing some of the symptoms of mild dehydration—dry mouth and a headache. A headache can also be caused when alcohol relaxes and enlarges the cranial vessels in the head.

What about fatigue and weakness? After much alcohol is consumed, the liver sets to work metabolizing the alcohol. The molecules that help the liver to metabolize the alcohol normally are processing other toxic materials, such as lactic acid. But as we have learned, when alcohol comes into the bloodstream, the liver focuses on it, allowing other dangerous toxins to begin to build up. A buildup of lactic acid in your muscles can make you feel exhausted and shaky.

The upset stomach and nausea that come with a hangover are most often caused by the increased amounts of acid your stomach has produced, which was triggered by alcohol. If you have already vomited, your stomach will be empty and even more acidic, making your stomach feel even queasier.

Finally, a kind of "rebound effect" is generally thought to contribute to the extreme sensitivity to light and sound that a hangover may cause. Your body is attempting to get back to normal. A lot of alcohol has reduced your body's sensitivity to different sources of stimulation, including light and sound. As the body attempts to bounce back to a normal state, you may feel even more sensitive to noises and sunlight.

This 22-year-old man, known to the San Francisco street community as "Shwill," claims to have started drinking with his mother as a young boy. Studies have suggested that adolescent drinkers are more vulnerable to the deleterious health effects of alcohol than adult drinkers.

DRUGS AND ALCOHOL DON'T MIX

There is one last element of alcohol's impact on your body that is important to remember, and that is the way that alcohol can interact with drugs and medications. Alcohol is a drug, and, if you are taking prescription, over-the-counter medications or any other drug, alcohol can drastically change the way the drug affects your body. In some cases, it can interfere with the drug; in other cases, it can greatly increase its effects.

One example is a common over-the-counter medication: antihistamines, which are used to treat colds or allergies. These types of medications can make you feel drowsy. When alcohol is added, the sleep-inducing aspect of the medication is greatly magnified.

The combination of alcohol and anti-anxiety medication

or sleeping medication—drugs such as Valium (diazepam)—can prove fatal. Such a combination severely depresses the central nervous system. Alcohol can dramatically increase the effects of many other drugs, causing their effect to be magnified many times.

THE FRENCH PARADOX

You may have heard someone say that they drink a glass or two of wine a day because it is good for them. In recent years, the media has popularized a theory that focuses on the low incidence of cardiovascular disease in France, in spite of a French diet that is rich in fats. This is known as the "French Paradox."

In the French Paradox, some researchers suggested that because the French diet traditionally involves drinking wine or alcohol, the wine was somehow providing protection against cardiovascular disease. This is, in a way, a throwback to the days when it was believed that alcohol provided useful medicinal purposes. Many studies have been carried out to determine why the French Paradox exists.

Some research has focused on the fact that red wine contains certain components called flavonoids and other antioxidants. Flavonoids are a type of plant compound that are found in a variety of fruits and vegetables and tea as well as in red wine. Certain studies have found that flavonoids improve health by their ability to combat oxidation. What is oxidation? Oxidation is a process in which substances that damage cells accumulate in the body. These cell-damaging substances are known as free radicals. When the free radicals accumulate in the body, leading to oxidation, the body shows an increased chance of developing heart disease and stroke as well as certain other diseases.

Conversely, research has suggested that when people consume more foods containing flavonoids, their risk of developing certain chronic diseases—such as heart disease, stroke, lung and prostate cancer, type-2 diabetes, and even asthma—drops. Those who support the connection between drinking red wine and a decreased risk of heart disease often point to the flavonoids the wine contains as an explanation for the French Paradox.

However, most experts believe that the lower incidence of cardiovascular disease in France cannot be explained simply by the drinking of wine. Rather, it is related to the French diet as a whole—a diet rich in fruits and fresh vegetables, many of which may also contain flavonoids and other antioxidants.

Other researchers also point out the differences in lifestyle that may contribute to an increased or decreased risk of developing heart disease. In France, the average work week is generally shorter than in the United States, and the vacation time employers offer is generally much more generous. More time is devoted to food preparation and consumption—there is less reliance on fast food and quick, convenient meals and more emphasis on fresh ingredients. There are many other lifestyle factors that may contribute to a person's chance of developing heart disease, including exercise and stress, none of which can be erased by a glass of red wine.

Nonetheless, research continues in order to determine the cause of the French Paradox and the possible connection between a glass of red wine and a lower incidence of heart disease.

THE BIG PICTURE

The effects we have discussed here are the short-term effects of alcohol, how a drink or several drinks travel through your body, affecting its ability to function normally. But there are even more serious effects that are caused when you drink steadily for longer periods of time.

One obvious effect is tolerance. Your body becomes accustomed to the alcohol. You require more and more alcohol to get the effect that a single drink used to give. Your liver has adapted

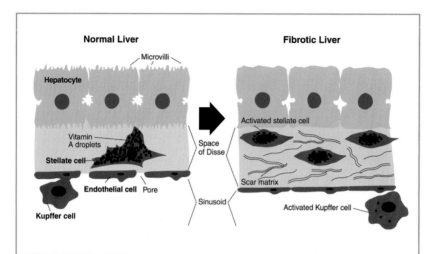

This comparison of a normal liver to a fibrotic liver demonstrates the mechanism through which cirrhosis develops. During fibrosis, stellate cells in the liver lose vitamin A and secrete scar tissue. This scar tissue interferes with the normal exchange of nutrients into and out of the sinusoid which is essential to maintaining a healthy liver. Activation of the Kupffer cells (specialized cells in the liver that destroy bacteria and worn-out blood cells) by alcohol may be responsible for starting this chain of events, which ultimately inhibits the normal functioning of the liver.

to the alcohol and now is able to metabolize it more quickly.

Alcohol can be addictive. If you drink steadily for long periods of time, your body does more than become accustomed to alcohol—it becomes dependent on it. Your body will experience symptoms of withdrawal when you stop drinking, such as shaking, sweating, vomiting, difficulty sleeping, and irritability.

Frequent drinking often damages the liver. Cirrhosis is one of the most common diseases of the liver caused by too much alcohol. Excessive alcohol causes the liver to become inflamed and diseased, and scar tissue develops. This condition cannot be corrected, and once cirrhosis develops, your body struggles to get rid of toxic substances. There is a much greater risk of early death. Inflammation of the liver may also lead to hepatitis.

Alcohol abuse damages more than just the liver. It damages brain cells and reduces the supply of blood to the brain. It robs the brain of vitamins that are necessary for proper brain functioning. It damages the central nervous system by affecting coordination, movement, and perception, as well as leading to loss of memory functioning. It can create confused and disorganized thinking.

Excessive alcohol consumption leads to premature aging. It can damage the digestive system, making it more difficult for the body to process nonalcoholic foods.

And research has shown that alcohol, even in small amounts (as little as one or two drinks), can greatly increase a pregnant woman's risk for having a baby with birth defects, for miscarriages, or for premature delivery. Why? In the same way that alcohol quickly travels through the body's fluids, it passes into the placenta (the organ within a pregnant woman that joins to the fetus). The developing unborn child has no tolerance for alcohol, and, worse, the impact of alcohol is much greater on a fetus's growth and development. When a developing fetus is exposed to alcohol, fetal alcohol syndrome may result. Its impact can be devastating and include symptoms and abnormalities like mental retardation, undersized head and brain, lack of proper height and weight growth, facial abnormalities, poorly formed organs, and overactive behavior.

4

Teenage Trends and Attitudes

It can be extremely difficult to be at a party or with a group of friends and be the only one who says "no" to something. We all want to fit in, to be accepted. Alcohol can seem like an easy way to be accepted. If everyone is drinking, you may feel uncomfortable being the only one choosing not to drink.

But is it true that "everybody" is drinking? Exactly who chooses to drink beer, wine, or other alcoholic beverages? And why?

WHO IS DRINKING?

According to a 2000 Gallup Poll, approximately 64 percent of all Americans are drinking alcoholic beverages—drinks like wine, beer, and other spirits. Approximately 36 percent of all Americans do not drink any alcohol (a group sometimes described as "teetotalers"). This may seem like a high number (more than half of all Americans are consuming some kind of alcoholic beverage), but it actually marks a decline from the late 1970s, when Gallup recorded that more than 70 percent of all Americans drank alcohol. More Americans drink beer than any other form of alcohol, according to the same poll. Wine came in second, followed by other forms of spirits.

But what about teens? Is it true that "everybody" is drinking? A study by MADD shows that approximately 50 percent of all 10th graders have had too much to drink at some time, whereas 41 percent of 9th graders have reported having tried alcohol at least once. But these experiments with alcohol come with a price tag: there

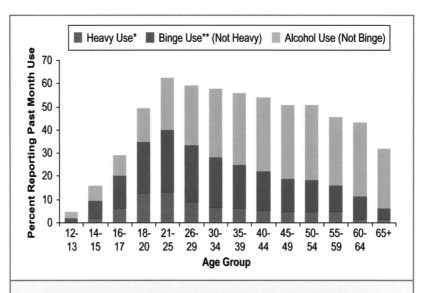

Heavy Use* Binge Use** (Not Heavy) Alcohol Use (Not Binge)

This graph from the 2000 National Household Survey on Drug Abuse (NHSDA) shows the pattern of alcohol use in different age groups. Binge drinking was defined as five or more drinks on a single occasion in the past month, and heavy drinking was defined as five or more drinks on a single occasion on five days in the past month.

is a relationship between students who drink and poor grades. In more than 40 percent students who have academic problems, alcohol is a factor. And alcohol is also a factor in 28 percent of all high-school dropouts.

Problems with alcohol aren't just limited to high-school students. A study by the Core Institute, *2000 Statistics on Alcohol and Other Drug Use on American Campuses*, notes that 23 percent of all college students who drank alcohol reported doing poorly on a test or project afterward, and more than 33 percent admit to missing classes because of alcohol use.

There are many other risks posed by alcohol. Alcohol is a leading cause of driving accidents for teens, as well as a factor in suicide, depression, and violent crimes involving teens. The earlier you start drinking, the more likely you are to become dependent on or abuse alcohol. Given all of these risks and dangers, why are teens drinking? Why are they choosing to use—and often abuse—alcohol?

WHY TEENS DRINK

It is difficult to pick specific characteristics of teens who decide to drink alcohol. But among heavy alcohol drinkers, there are certain common traits—factors that should alarm any teen who drinks alcohol:

- Heavy teen drinkers (those who consume five or more alcoholic beverages when they drink) are twice as likely as nondrinkers to say their schoolwork is poor.

- Heavy teen drinkers are four to six times more likely to say that they cut classes or skip school.

- Heavy teen drinkers are three times more likely to say that they deliberately try to hurt or kill themselves and twice as likely to say that they think about committing suicide.

Heavy teen drinkers create problems for others as well as for themselves. Studies have clearly shown that alcohol use and abuse lead to aggressive behavior. Teens who drink frequently and heavily are more likely to run away from home, to steal (from home and elsewhere), and to physically attack other people and their property. They are more likely to get into fights, to shoplift, and to break the law. All of these dangerous behaviors are in addition to the threat posed by anyone who has been drinking and then gets behind the wheel of a car.

A team of researchers at the University of California at San Diego has recently uncovered some alarming facts about how alcohol abuse can prove particularly dangerous for the brain functioning of teens. During adolescence, critical brain development is taking place, particularly for brain nerve cell connections. Cerebral metabolic rates are high until you reach the age of about 20. Because of this, alcohol affects teens

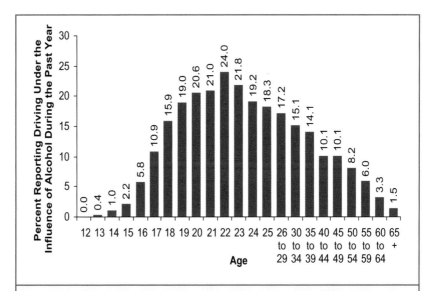

This graph from the 2000 NHSDA shows the percentage of people in different age groups who reported driving under the influence of alcohol. Many people believe they will never get behind the wheel after drinking, but alcohol impairs judgment and may make someone who has been drinking believe he or she is not impaired.

differently from the way it affects adults. It can damage memory function, making it much more difficult for the brain to retain information. These effects are true not only for the period in time when you are drinking, but continue to damage your brain long after the party has ended.

SPECIAL RISKS FOR GIRLS

Drinking poses risks for both male and female teens, but alcohol can create unique problems for girls. Because male teens usually weigh more and have more body water than female teens, alcohol becomes more diluted in the bodies of male drinkers. Female drinkers generally have higher concentrations of alcohol in their blood than male drinkers, even when they have consumed precisely the same amount of alcohol.

Tracy finds school useless and boring. The teachers stand at the front of the classroom writing numbers or words on the blackboard, while the students whisper, pass notes, or just stare off into space. Things aren't much better at home. Her parents get home late from work, pour themselves a beer, and then either fight with each other or stare at the television. Tracy feels invisible. When she drinks, she doesn't mind feeling invisible. She can sit in the middle of the buzzing classroom and daydream about being somewhere else. She can stare at the television with her parents and imagine she is in the middle of whatever make-believe world they are watching on the screen.

Sometimes it seems to Colin that he and his friends drink because there's nothing better to do. He doesn't remember exactly when they started. They were hanging out at somebody's house the way they always did, but this time somebody had brought a six-pack of beer. After that, they almost always had alcohol when they got together. If they didn't, they were talking about ways to get it. Sometimes somebody brought a bottle of cheap wine; other times, beer. Once one of Colin's friends brought a bottle of something that made them all sick—Colin couldn't even remember what it was, but it had really made the room spin. The stuff was easy enough to get. The boys looked older than their age, and they soon figured out which stores didn't ask for ID.

Some people, like Tracy and Colin, use alcohol to escape from the pain of everyday life, to combat boredom, or to fit in with their friends. Although alcohol provides a temporary solution to these problems—it may, in fact, make you feel better while you're intoxicated—what these teens don't know is that alcohol use can create more problems than it solves. Tracy and Colin are putting themselves at risk for developing psychological problems like depression and learning difficulties.

Teenage girls who are heavy drinkers are more likely to engage in sexual intercourse and less likely to use condoms, resulting in greater risk of unwanted pregnancy and sexually transmitted disease, including HIV and AIDS. Females are among the fastest-growing portion of the U.S. population to become infected with HIV, and teens are particularly at risk.

Teen girls who drink regularly should be aware that menstrual problems can result from heavy drinking—problems like increased menstrual flow, greater pain and discomfort, irregular periods, or even problems that will make it more difficult to have a baby later in life.

Daughters of alcoholics face a special risk. Studies have shown that if your parents abuse alcohol, you are more likely to become an alcoholic yourself and to marry a man who is an alcoholic.

Alcohol also plays a factor in sexual assaults and so-called "date rape." It's not enough to simply say "no"; you must be aware that if you are at a party or event where others are drinking, alcohol can lead to aggressive behavior—behavior that may threaten you or someone you care about.

CHOOSING TO SAY "NO"

Of course, it can be awkward and uncomfortable to be the only one at a party who isn't drinking. If you know that you are going to be somewhere where alcohol is being served and you don't want to drink, it can help to be prepared to say no. Think about why you don't want to drink. Imagine the scene in your head, and practice feeling confident about your choice not to drink.

The National Institute on Alcohol Abuse and Alcoholism has prepared some ways to say "no" to alcohol. You may find some of these helpful:

- No thanks, I want to stay in control.
- No thanks, I am driving.
- No thanks, I don't want to get into trouble with my parents.

These teens volunteer for Connecticut Coalition to Stop Underage Drinking, which creates sting operations designed to identify those who sell liquor to minors.

- No thanks, if I drink I'll lose my privileges (the car, be grounded, etc.)
- No thanks, I don't like the way it tastes.
- No thanks, I've got to study later (or get up early, or pick up somebody, or . . .)
- No thanks, drinking makes me tired.
- No thanks, I'm trying to lose weight.
- No thanks, I'm in training.
- No thanks, what else have you got?
- No thanks, I don't drink.

There is no "right" or "wrong" way to refuse alcohol. You can come up with your own "no thanks" or use one of the ones suggested here. You may find it helpful to get some support from a family member or friend. You can share your concerns and get some help and encouragement.

TOP 10 MYTHS ABOUT DRINKING

Sometimes it's hard to separate fact from fiction when you're talking about alcohol. The National Institute on Alcohol Abuse and Alcoholism, as well as organizations such as MADD, regularly post information on their websites that demonstrates the dangers of drinking in addition to providing a clearer picture of how alcohol can affect you and the people around you. Their websites, as well as other useful sources of information about alcohol, are listed at the back of this book.

Many myths about alcohol circulate among teens and adults. The more you drink, the more likely you are to have believed one of these myths yourself. Take a look at these myths about alcohol and see if any of them sound like something you may have been told or believe about alcohol:

- Myth #1:   Drinking isn't that dangerous.
- Myth #2:   I can drink without it affecting me.
- Myth #3:   I can sober up quickly with a cup of coffee or a cold shower.
- Myth #4:   I have to drink to hang with my friends.
- Myth #5:   Beer isn't as dangerous as "stronger" drinks.
- Myth #6:   I'm a good driver, even if I've had something to drink.
- Myth #7:   Alcohol gives me energy.
- Myth #8:   It's only alcohol. It's not like I'm using drugs.
- Myth #9:   If I drink too much, the worst that will happen is a bad hangover.
- Myth #10: So what if I drink? It's my body—I'm only hurting myself.

Have you heard any of these myths? Maybe from yourself or your friends? Let's take a look at the real facts.

Myth #1: Drinking isn't that dangerous. One out of every three older teens admitted to a hospital emergency room for a serious injury is intoxicated. Alcohol is a major factor in all automobile accidents involving teens. And when alcohol is involved, there is a greater risk of suicide, homicide, or drowning.

Myth #2: I can drink without it affecting me. Drinking affects your judgment—your ability to make good decisions—whether you're aware of it or not. Once that happens, you're more likely to do something you'll regret, such as having unprotected sex, damaging someone's property, or being victimized by someone else.

Myth #3: I can sober up quickly with a cup of coffee or a

DRINKING AND DEPRESSION: THE STRAIGHT FACTS

Terms like "Happy Hour" and stereotypes of the cheerful drunk at a holiday party can make you believe that drinking will help you feel happier. But take a look at this survey of teen drinkers (aged 12 to 17) to see how they are really feeling:

- Nearly half of all teens who drank alcohol reported feeling lonely.

- Approximately 30 percent of all teens who drank said that they cried a lot.

- More than 10 percent of all teens who drank reported deliberately trying to hurt or kill themselves.

- More than 20 percent of all teens who drank said that they felt as if no one loved them.

- More than 16 percent of all teens who drank felt worthless or inferior.

Source: "Patterns of Alcohol Use Among Adolescents and Associations with Emotional and Behavioral Problems," Office of Applied Studies Working Paper, Substance Abuse and Mental Health Services Administration, March 2000

cold shower. Depending on how much you weigh and how much you have had to eat, it can take two to three hours to eliminate the alcohol in your body from only one to two drinks. Nothing can speed up the process. Coffee, cold showers, and exercise make no difference at all.

Myth #4: I have to drink to hang with my friends. Each person handles alcohol differently. Females process alcohol differently than males. You cannot measure how alcohol will affect you by watching how it affects your friends. Nor should you let anyone tell you when or how much to drink.

Myth #5: Beer isn't as dangerous as "stronger" drinks. There is just as much alcohol in a 12-ounce bottle of beer as in a five-ounce glass of wine or a standard shot of 80-proof liquor (whether in a mixed drink or straight). Alcohol affects your body, no matter how you drink it.

Myth #6: I'm a good driver, even if I've had something to drink. Alcohol impairs your judgment. You may think you're driving well, without realizing how the alcohol has affected your response time and coordination. Underage drinking is illegal, and if you are caught drinking and driving you could lose your license. More important, teen drivers who have been drinking have a much greater risk of having a fatal car crash than nondrinkers.

Myth #7: Alcohol gives me energy. Alcohol is a depressant. It actually slows you down, affecting your ability to think, move, and speak.

Myth #8: It's only alcohol. It's not like I'm using drugs. Alcohol *is* a drug. More than twice as many people are killed by alcohol and tobacco than by cocaine, heroin, and all other illegal drugs—combined.

Myth #9: If I drink too much, the worst that will happen is a bad hangover. If you drink too much too quickly, you can literally poison your body and die in only a few hours.

Myth #10: So what if I drink? It's my body—I'm only hurting myself. If you drink, you put many more people than

This vehicle was involved in a drunk driving accident. The National Transportation and Safety Administration estimates that 519,000 people, or one person per minute, are injured in alcohol-related crashes every year.

yourself at risk. Drinking can lead to aggressive behavior—behavior that can damage other people and their property. Innocent people have been killed because of drunk drivers. Alcohol damages many more people than simply the person with the drink in his or her hand.

We've explored some of the facts and fiction about alcohol, as well as ways for you to make responsible decisions about alcohol. Let's next take a look at the problems you might face if you suspect that someone you care about—a family member or friend—is drinking too much and how you can help.

5

Alcoholism:
Identifying the Disease

What do you do when you believe that someone you care about is drinking too much? Is there anything you can say or do that will help them to recognize how destructive their behavior is? How do you know if someone you love is an alcoholic? And what can you do to help?

Alcohol is a drug that affects not simply the person who is using it, but many other people as well. The Children of Alcoholics Foundation estimates that 7 million children under the age of 18 are growing up in an alcoholic family in the United States. And there are many teens who know someone—a friend or relative—who is struggling with an addiction to alcohol.

Is there anything you can do to help someone who is abusing alcohol? Let's take a look at some of the realities about alcohol and its impact on family members and friends.

WHO IS AN ALCOHOLIC?
An alcoholic is someone who is struggling with alcoholism—a disease that occurs from excessive consumption of alcoholic beverages. It is the "excessive consumption" that marks the difference between someone who may be referred to as a "social drinker" and someone who regularly abuses alcohol. You can think of alcoholism as what happens when drinking alcohol begins to cause damage to the drinker and/or to others.

Who precisely can be described as an alcoholic? Alcoholics

Alcoholism is a disease that results from the continued and excessive consumption of alcoholic drinks. An alcoholic is not always the stereotypical "drunk" portrayed by the media, but may function very well for a time despite the disease.

Anonymous often describes an alcoholic as a person who cannot accurately predict what will happen when he or she takes a drink, and it refers to alcoholism as an "obsession of the mind and an allergy of the body." There is a mental as well as a physical aspect of alcoholism, and both are important

Karen dreaded coming home from school. She was never sure what she would find. Sometimes she could hear the television, or music blaring from the stereo, before she even reached her front door. Noise generally meant trouble—it meant that her mother had been drinking again. Silence was good—it meant that her mother had been able to keep her job for another day and was still working. But lately, it seemed as if there were more bad days than good. Her mother was finding it harder and harder to keep a job, and recently there had been more and more afternoons when Karen came home to a noisy apartment and her mother slumped on the couch with a glass nearby.

Mark was worried about his girlfriend, Lori. He had begun to notice that every time they went to a party, she was looking for something to drink—something with alcohol in it—the minute they arrived. Sometimes when they went out—just the two of them—she brought some beer that she had smuggled out of her parents' house. He felt that he had to drink when he was with her—she was his girlfriend after all, and he was a guy. He couldn't let a girl drink more than he did. And he knew that her family was having problems. Her parents were getting a divorce. Mark wanted to help Lori, but he didn't know what to do or say. He did know that he didn't like the way Lori acted after she had been drinking. It made her more sensitive to everything he said and did. Sometimes she would snap for no apparent reason. And then she would fall asleep in his car when he was driving her home. Lately it seemed that they didn't do any of the things they used to do. Lori only wanted to hang out and drink.

Karen and Mark are faced with the difficult task of helping a loved one recognize a drinking problem. Alcoholism is a disease suffered by an individual, but the symptoms of the disease affect everyone in the alcoholic's life. And just as untrained people like Karen and Mark wouldn't be expected to treat a family member's cancer, they have to realize that their alcoholic loved ones will most likely need to seek help from a doctor, a therapist, or a group like Alcoholics Anonymous.

to keep in mind when thinking about alcoholism and alcoholics. An alcoholic generally continues to drink in spite of the problems that it will cause to himself or herself—and to others.

A DISEASE, NOT A WEAKNESS

An important change in the way people viewed alcoholism began to take place in the middle of the twentieth century. Before that, alcoholics were more commonly referred to as "drunks," and alcoholism was viewed more as a character flaw, weakness, or sin rather than a disease.

But studies and research in the mid-twentieth century began to change this way of thinking. It began to become clear that many different factors contributed to a person's tendency to become an alcoholic, and that alcoholism was a disease—a disease that could be treated, but a disease that required care from a rehabilitation facility, hospital, or other professional setting.

Most experts feel that alcoholism should be viewed as a chronic disease. A chronic disease is different from an illness like the flu. A chronic disease is an illness that recurs—once you have it, you have it for life. It may be treatable, but there is no cure. You need to learn to live with the illness, to manage it. Another factor of a chronic disease is the pace of its development. Unlike the flu, you don't simply wake up one morning suffering from alcoholism. It develops slowly, over time, and there are clues that mark the pace of the illness.

FOUR STAGES OF ALCOHOLISM

E.M. Jellinek, one of the earliest researchers to focus on the study of alcohol and alcoholism, outlined four stages that mark the progress of alcoholism. According to Jellinek, alcoholism begins with what he called a prealcoholic phase—a time when drinking takes place during social occasions. Drinking brings stress relief, and soon the individual begins to look for situations in which drinking will take place. The second phase occurs when the drinker begins to suffer "blackouts." He or she seems to be functioning, but later has no memory of what happened. He or she may sneak an extra drink before a party or quickly gulp the first drink or two. The third phase Jellinek described as the crucial phase—a time when the individual can control whether he or she takes a drink, but once drinking begins the individual cannot stop. The fourth and final stage is the chronic phase, a period during which drinking occurs almost every day, almost all day long.

The last and chronic phase seems the bleakest, but it is actually a time when someone who drinks may be willing to seek help. They may recognize that they are not in control, that they cannot manage their drinking, and be willing to find a way to regain control of their lives.

FOCUS ON THE FAMILY

If you grow up in a family where alcohol is abused, are you more likely to develop an addiction to alcohol yourself? The answer is yes. In studies of both male and female alcoholics, researchers found that between 25 and 50 percent had an alcoholic family member. It is not simply a matter of alcohol being present in the house or regularly witnessing a parent or other family member abusing alcohol. Studies of adopted children born to alcoholic parents have revealed that even if children were adopted by age six weeks into a family in which alcohol was not regularly consumed, those whose natural parents were alcoholic were more likely to become alcoholics. Clearly, a genetic or biological factor contributes to whether or not a person ultimately becomes an alcoholic. This means that you need to be aware that having an alcoholic parent makes you more at risk for developing a problem with alcohol.

Research is ongoing to determine precisely what genetically contributes to the development of alcoholism.

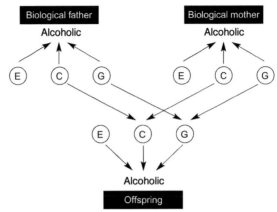

A. Influences on offspring alcoholism in an intact nuclear family

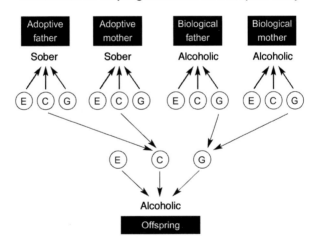

B. Influences on offspring alcoholism in an adoptive family

This diagram compares the contributions of genetic (G), common environmental (C), and non-shared environmental (E) factors on the development of alcoholism between parents and children in an intact nuclear family and an adoptive family. Genetic factors seem to be the most important in the development of alcoholism, as children of alcoholics, even if adopted by sober adoptive parents, still have a greater chance of developing alcoholism.

LIFE WITH AN ALCOHOLIC

If you have a friend or family member who is abusing alcohol, you may not be aware of the ways in which their drinking affects your behavior. In a family with a parent abusing alcohol, this parent is unable to fulfill his or her "normal" functions. Often other people step into the gap to take care of what isn't being done. Because alcoholics are undependable and their behavior is unpredictable, family members and friends of alcoholics may feel as if they are "walking on eggshells"—trying to carefully avoid doing or saying anything that may upset the alcoholic or cause him or her to reach for a drink.

Living in an alcoholic home can make relationships nearly impossible and place a heavy burden on the teen whose parent or friend is suffering from alcoholism. You may be reluctant to invite friends to your home if you have a parent whose behavior has been affected by alcohol. You may feel that you need to "fill in" for an alcoholic parent—by phoning the job to say that he or she is "sick" and can't come to work or by cooking or shopping or caring for younger brothers and sisters. You may feel as if you need to constantly watch what you say or do to avoid upsetting a parent who has had too much to drink. Or, you may become accustomed to the fact that a parent may not show up when expected—at your football game, to pick you up from school, or for an important event. This kind of behavior is called enabling.

Enabling means that you "enable"—or make it possible—for the alcoholic person to continue to abuse alcohol without being forced to confront the true consequences of his or her actions. Your family continues to function because everybody fills in the gaps or changes how they would otherwise behave in order to accommodate the person who has been drinking.

The same thing is true when the alcoholic is not a member of your family but someone you care about—a boyfriend or girlfriend or a close friend. Enabling their behavior doesn't necessarily mean that you're the one who pours the drinks or drives to a place where the person can drink. It means that you make it possible for someone you care about to continue to abuse alcohol. Perhaps you share your notes or the details of the homework assignment if he or she falls asleep in class or misses class altogether. Maybe you let a friend spend the night at your house to prevent the friend's parents from finding out about their son's or daughter's drinking. Maybe you explain away your girlfriend's drunken behavior at a party by telling others that she's been under a lot of stress lately. Perhaps you excuse a boyfriend's violence or angry outbursts by blaming yourself. These are all signs that you are making it possible for someone you care about to continue to do something that is hurting them—and could hurt others.

Remember that you are not really helping your friend. By

ALCOHOLISM IN THE FAMILY: THE STRAIGHT FACTS

If you are living in a family where someone is abusing alcohol, you can feel as if your family is completely different from any other you know. It is important to remember that you can get help, and that you are not alone. In fact, many people report having an alcoholic family member or dealing with family issues surrounding alcohol abuse:

- About 43 percent of all adults in the U.S. (approximately 76 million Americans) say that they have been exposed to alcoholism in their family.

- Nearly one out of every five adults (18 percent) in the U.S. lived with an alcoholic while growing up.

- There are nearly 27 million children of alcoholics living in the U.S. Research suggests that more than 11 million of them are under the age of 18.

[Source: National Association for Children of Alcoholics]

taking on your friend's responsibilities or by accommodating his or her moods, you are preventing your friend from beginning to get help for the disease.

HOW CAN I TELL IF MY FRIEND HAS A PROBLEM?

People who are drinking too much can find it difficult to recognize that they are no longer in control. They may not appreciate how their drinking is affecting others, and they may believe that they are in control.

How can you tell if a friend or someone you care about has a problem with alcohol? The Harvard School of Public Health has put together a checklist of warning signs. If your friend has one or more of the following symptoms, he or she may have a problem with alcohol:

- He or she gets drunk on a regular basis.
- He or she lies about how much alcohol they have been drinking.
- The person you care about avoids activities he or she used to enjoy in order to get drunk.
- He or she avoids you in order to get drunk.
- He or she plans drinking in advance, hides alcohol, or drinks alone.
- He or she has to drink more to get the same high.
- He or she believes that you need to drink in order to have fun.
- He or she frequently suffers hangovers.
- He or she pressures others to drink.
- The person you care about forgets what he or she did while drinking.
- He or she drinks and drives.
- He or she has been suspended from school—or fired from a job—for an alcohol-related incident.
- He or she takes risks, including sexual risks.
- He or she constantly talks about drinking.
- He or she is feeling run-down, hopeless, depressed, or even suicidal.

Binge drinking, defined as 5 or more alcoholic drinks consumed on one occasion, is often encouraged in social situations throughout high school and college. Researchers at Duke University hypothesize that binge drinking may pose a special risk to adolescents, like learning difficulties and memory loss.

WHAT YOU CAN DO

People drink for many different reasons, and for many people, little happens beyond the occasional hangover or upset stomach. But for some people who are biologically and mentally geared in a particular way, the occasional drink quickly gives way to drinking often and in large quantities.

For these people, drinking soon becomes the focus of their thoughts and actions. Without help, they can develop serious psychological problems (things like depression and suicidal thoughts) and serious physical problems (liver disease, brain damage). Their drinking may affect their ability to make good choices about issues like safe sex, and unsafe sex may lead to an unwanted pregnancy or a sexually transmitted disease like AIDS.

People who drink may tell you that drinking is helping them to cope or to feel better. But alcohol affects their judgment—their ability to tell whether or not they are truly feeling better or worse. When they stop drinking, they will become more depressed.

When you think of a person who is an alcoholic, you may not think about a person your own age. Teens often believe that becoming addicted will never happen to them. They often deny that they have a problem with alcohol. They may refuse to admit that anything is wrong—or not even recognize that they are drinking too much.

Although you cannot force someone to admit that there is a problem or force him or her to stop drinking, there are certain things you can do to help someone you care about who is abusing alcohol. The first thing you can do is talk to someone you can trust about your friend's problem—perhaps a counselor, a teacher, a doctor, or a parent. Ask them to keep what you are sharing confidential. You don't even need to mention your friend's name. Adults can often provide you with additional resources or information that may be helpful while you decide what to do next.

If you decide to talk to the person you believe is drinking too much, think carefully in advance about what you want to say and when you want to say it. Pick a time when the person has not been drinking. Don't call him an alcoholic or blame him for his drinking; rather, let him know that you are concerned. Tell him how his drinking makes you feel. Tell him what you've seen when he's been drinking—specific things you've seen him do or say that bothered you. Make it clear that you are talking to him because you care.

Be prepared that your friend or family member may become angry, make excuses, or deny what you are saying. Stress that you are speaking because you are worried. Offer to go with your friend or family member to get help.

HELP IS AVAILABLE

There are certain groups and organizations that specialize in helping family members and friends of alcoholics. These groups can offer you support and advice. Your phone book contains a list of local organizations that specialize in issues surrounding alcohol abuse. Your school nurse and counselor may also have information about support groups.

Certain national organizations may also have chapters or groups that meet in your area or may be able to provide you with information or even support. Some groups specialize in helping teens. You may want to begin with one of the groups listed at the end of Chapter 7.

6

Alcoholism:
Treating the Disease

One of alcohol's dangers is the way it affects your judgment. You may be abusing alcohol, drinking too much and too often, and yet not be able to realize that you have a problem. If you think that alcoholism is something that can happen only to someone else, someone older or somehow different from you, think again. Nobody is too young to have a problem with alcohol. Being addicted to alcohol doesn't depend on what kind of alcohol you've been drinking or how long you've been drinking. What matters is how the alcohol is affecting you.

There may have been some clues that you are developing a problem with alcohol. Perhaps a friend has told you that you are drinking too much, or told you that he or she is worried about your drinking. Maybe a boyfriend or girlfriend has been angry with you because of your drinking. Or, maybe the clues are coming from you—maybe you are feeling guilty because of your drinking or because of something that happened when you were drinking. Or, you are finding it harder and harder to get through the day without a drink, or you are spending more time thinking about drinking than anything else.

Some experts use a questionnaire known as CAGE to determine whether or not a person is suffering from a problem with alcohol. One or more "yes" answers indicates that there is a risk of alcohol abuse and dependence:

C Have you ever felt you should Cut down on your drinking?

A Have people Annoyed you by criticizing your drinking?

G Have you ever felt bad or Guilty about your drinking?

E Have you ever had a drink first thing in the morning (Eye opener)?

It can be difficult to recognize—or admit—that you have a problem. The organization Alcoholics Anonymous (AA) has developed a simple quiz for teenagers which you can find at *www.alcoholics-anonymous.org.* If you answer "yes" to one or

A t almost every party Lauren had gone to during the summer after her junior year of high school, beer had been served. She was proud of the fact that she could "hold her liquor," as one of the boys had said. She could drink a lot and almost never got sick. But lately she had found that sometimes she wouldn't remember all of what had happened the next day after a night of drinking. It was as if parts of her memory had been wiped away. Friends would tell her funny stories about things she had said or done, and she wouldn't remember doing or saying any of those things. Once or twice she had ended up with guys that she wouldn't even have talked to if she hadn't been drinking. Now, her best friend had told her that she thought Lauren was drinking too much—she had even called her an alcoholic! Lauren had laughed. She just liked drinking—she was way too young to be an alcoholic. Besides, she could stop anytime she wanted to. She just didn't want to right now.

Lauren may think she can stop drinking at any time, but she is starting to exhibit some of the warning signs of alcoholism—blackouts, memory loss, and poor judgment. Alcoholism does not discriminate, and can affect anyone of any age.

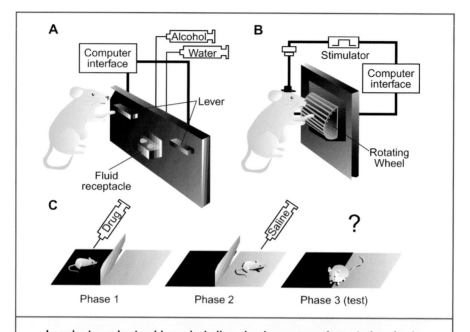

In order to understand how alcoholism develops, researchers study animals in situations that mimic the positive and negative reinforcing characteristics of alcohol. In situation A, a mouse is trained to push a lever to receive either alcohol or water. The mouse will push the alcohol lever enough times to become intoxicated. In situation B, the mouse is allowed to turn a wheel to receive an electrical current that produces pleasant feelings. In situation C, the mouse is trained to associate one test area (Phase 1) with a drug, another test area (Phase 2) with a non-drug, and then allowed to choose between the two areas (Phase 3). The mouse always chose Phase 1 test area—the drug. These tests indicate that receiving positive reinforcement from the good feelings produced by drugs like alcohol conditions the mouse to seek alcohol on subsequent occasions.

more of these questions, you may need to take a closer look at your drinking and how alcohol is affecting your life.

If your answers to these questions suggest that you have a problem with alcohol, there are many people and organizations that can help. Find someone you can trust—a teacher, school counselor, pastor, or parent—and ask for his or her advice. Look in your phone book for a list of local support groups and chapters of national organizations that may be able to provide you with information or assistance. At the end of this book you will also find a list of national organizations that specialize in providing information and assistance to teens and others struggling with alcohol-related problems.

TREATING THE PROBLEM

Many different treatment options are available for people struggling to overcome an addiction to alcohol. There are counselors who specialize in treating people suffering from alcohol-related problems. They focus not merely on the problem (alcohol) but on the person as a whole—his or her lifestyle (and ways to shift it away from alcohol-related activities); creating new ways to cope with stress; psychological problems that may have contributed to a dependence on alcohol; the physical symptoms and problems that can result from alcohol abuse; the chronic nature of alcoholism (meaning that treatment needs to contain an ongoing program to help the person continue to stay away from alcohol); and any concerns about relationships that may have been affected by alcohol (family and friends). Counselors may work with an individual, a group of people struggling with alcohol abuse, or a family that has been affected by the alcoholism of one or more members.

There are also organizations that specialize in assisting individuals struggling with alcoholism and other alcohol-related problems. One of the most famous of these is AA. AA began in Akron, Ohio, in 1935. An alcoholic known as Bill W. had a spiritual experience that led him to give up drinking, but one year later, while traveling through Akron, he suddenly had an overwhelming desire to have a drink. He decided instead to try to find another alcoholic who was struggling to stay sober. This first meeting of alcoholics struggling to stay away from temptation was the birth of what would become a world-wide organization. By 1939, the organization had grown to some 100 members, who published what they had done to stay sober in a book known as *Alcoholics Anonymous*. Today, there are more than 2 million members.

The principles on which AA is based rely on complete abstinence; in other words, if you are an alcoholic, the only way you can get better is by staying away from alcohol. AA defines sobriety as a critical goal—one that cannot be achieved simply by not drinking at any particular moment, but one that requires a more detailed, all-encompassing change. The change requires specific actions, known in AA as The Twelve Steps. These Twelve Steps, listed at *www.alcoholics-anonymous.org*, were not developed by professional counselors or therapists; they date back to the earliest days of AA and reveal what those original members did to stay sober.

THE TWELVE STEPS

Newcomers to AA meetings are not forced to follow all the Twelve Steps if they are unable or unwilling to do so. They are simply asked to keep an open mind, to attend meetings, and to read AA literature. AA relies on the concept that recovering alcoholics are in a unique position to help each other—that people who have been able to achieve sobriety are able to provide assistance and support to others who are struggling to stay sober. AA meetings are held around the country and throughout the world, in schools, churches, and other public places. Members share their struggles and the story of their problem drinking and then describe the sobriety they have achieved. New members are partnered with a more experienced member, who serves as a contact or "sponsor" to help support the new member's struggle to achieve sobriety.

AL-ANON AND ALATEEN

AA's success has led to two additional groups being formed. One of these, Al-Anon, offers support to family members of an alcoholic. The goal is to offer assistance and advice to

Alcoholics Anonymous is an organization dedicated to helping alcoholics stay sober through a Twelve Step program. The approach, outlined in AA's "Big Book," calls for complete abstinence from alcohol and a revised lifestyle. AA members, like the man in this picture, attend meetings and receive support from other recovering alcoholics in an anonymous setting.

family members and to help them understand how best to respond to the presence of an alcoholic in their family and how to focus on changing themselves rather than focusing on the drinker as the cause of all family problems. Alateen is another outgrowth of AA and Al-Anon. It specifically focuses on the concerns of teens dealing with an alcoholic family member or friend. Both Alateen and Al-Anon offer the benefit of a safe, confidential place to meet and share problems, to understand that you are not alone, and to learn more about the illness of alcoholism.

Al-Anon and Alateen members also have sponsors, attend meetings, and follow the Twelve Steps (understanding that they are powerless about someone else's drinking rather than their

STATISTICS ON ALCOHOL ABUSE: THE STRAIGHT FACTS

- Approximately 14 million Americans (more than seven percent of the population) meet the criteria for alcoholism or alcohol abuse.

- More than one-half of American adults have a close family member who is an alcoholic or has suffered from alcoholism.

- Approximately one out of every four children and teens under the age of 18 in the United States is exposed to alcohol abuse or dependence in his or her family.

- Of the more than 11 million victims of violent crime each year, almost one in four report that the offender had been drinking alcohol prior to committing the crime.

- The estimated cost of alcohol abuse was $184.6 billion for 1998 alone, or roughly $638 for every man, woman and child living in the United States that year.

[Source: 10th Special Report to the U.S. Congress on Alcohol and Health]

own). Currently more than 26,000 Al-Anon and Alateen groups are meeting in 115 countries.

OTHER SOURCES OF TREATMENT AND SUPPORT

In addition to individual therapy and support groups such as AA, other treatment options are available for people struggling with alcohol abuse. There are treatment centers around the country specifically designed for assisting people struggling with a dependency on alcohol or drugs. Here, patients live at the facility for a fixed period of time, where professionals are available for counseling and group meetings offer an opportunity for regular support from others struggling to overcome addictions. There are also outpatient facilities in which patients do not live at the treatment center but regularly come for assistance and treatment.

A report published by the U.S. Department of Health and Human Services in 2000 notes that every day, more than 700,000 people in the United States receive treatment for alcoholism. Doctors or nurses can often provide a useful first step in treatment. If you feel comfortable talking with your health care provider, he or she may be able to provide you with details of appropriate treatment options in your area.

TREATMENT WITH MEDICATION

Research is under way that focuses on the possible treatment of alcohol dependence with medications. Since 1995, scientists have focused on the development of new drugs to treat alcoholism—drugs that focus on the molecular level of the brain processes that promote and maintain addiction.

Studies have shown that the multiple chemical messenger systems in the brain, called neurotransmitter systems, are involved in cases of problem drinking. Treatment options involving medication focus on these different neurotransmitter systems.

One of these is a group of drugs called opiate antagonists.

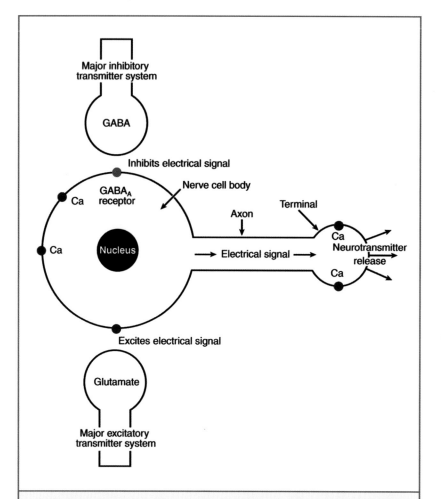

This diagram of a nerve cell (neuron) shows the major neurochemical systems affected by alcohol. Alcohol slows down the electrical activity of a nerve cell by enhancing a neurotransmitter (a chemical messenger) known as GABA; GABA inhibits electrical activity. Alcohol also inhibits another neurotransmitter known as glutamate. Glutamate slows the flow of calcium (Ca) into cells, which is essential for normal cell function. Without calcium, neurotransmitters at the end of the neuron (on the right side of this diagram) will not be released normally, and the electrical impulse that should travel from this neuron to the next neuron will be slowed. This process is part of a chain of events in the brain that creates the behaviors associated with alcohol intoxication.

These medications interfere with neurotransmitter systems that produce feelings of pleasure when alcohol is used. Patients taking opiate antagonists do not get the expected pleasant "high" from alcohol. Two of these medications, naltrexone and nalmefene, may prove to be promising in treating alcohol dependence.

Other research has focused on medications that affect different neurotransmitter systems—those involved in maintaining a dependence on alcohol. The hope is that these may help break the cycle of dependence that often causes alcoholics to relapse after they have stopped drinking for a period of time. Additional research concentrates on the effects of a combination of these two types of medications in an effort to reduce both the risk of heavy drinking and the risk of relapse.

Other medications may treat not only alcoholism itself, but some of the conditions that may have sparked it in the first place. Antidepressants make up one class of drugs that has proved helpful in combating the depression that often leads to alcohol abuse or follows period of heavy drinking.

While medication offers great promise, most experts believe that psychological treatment is equally critical for alcohol-related problems. A combination of the two may prove helpful to people suffering from severe alcoholism.

7

Exploring Additional Resources

We have discussed how alcohol can affect your body. We have learned a bit about the history of alcohol, particularly in the United States. We have examined some of the legal issues surrounding alcohol use and how those laws have changed in the past 100 years.

We have read about teens making decisions about alcohol and learned more about who is likely to abuse alcohol and why. We have taken a look at some of the myths surrounding alcohol and discovered how, just like any drug, it can become addictive. We have discussed alcohol addiction and learned about some of the ways to prevent alcohol-related problems from forming. Most important, we have talked about what to do if you or a friend or family member needs help with an alcohol problem.

Many resources are available if you need assistance, support, or just more information about alcohol. Start with the adults you know. A parent, a teacher, your school counselor, a minister, or your physician or nurse may be able to provide support or suggestions for places where you will find the help you need. There are also a number of organizations that specialize in dealing with alcohol-related issues, offering support groups, counseling, an on-line network or helpful statistics and information. Many of these may have local chapters in your area—you can check your phone book to find one near you.

RESOURCES ON ALCOHOL

Al-Anon Family Groups
(for information on Alcoholics Anonymous, Al-Anon, and Alateen)
Address: 1600 Corporate Landing Parkway, Virginia Beach,
VA 23454
Telephone: (for meeting information across the country):
1-888-425-2666
Websites:
www.alcoholicsanonymous.org (Alcoholics Anonymous),
www.al-anon.org (Al-Anon—for families of alcoholics),
www.alateen.org (Alateen—for teens with an alcoholic
family member or friend)

Center for Substance Abuse Research (CESAR)
Offers fact sheets on drug and alcohol use, information on specific
alcohol-related issues, and links to major surveys.
Address: 4321 Hartwick Rd., Suite 501, College Park,
MD 20740
Telephone: 1-301-403-8329
Website: www.cesar.umd.edu

Children of Alcoholics Foundation
Does not hold meetings, but gives out information and offers an
e-mail support network for teens.
Address: 164 W. 74th Street, New York, NY 10023
Telephone: 1-212-595-5810, ext. 7760
Web site: www.coaf.org

Families Anonymous
A support group for relatives and friends of those who have drug,
alcohol, or behavioral problems.
Address: P.O. Box 3475, Culver City, CA 90231-3475
Telephone: 1-800-736-9805
Website: www.familiesanonymous.org

Go Ask Alice

A website run by Columbia University that provides details on a wide range of health-related issues, including alcohol and drug use.

Address: Alice!, Lerner Hall, Columbia University, 2920 Broadway, 7th Floor, New York, NY 10027

Telephone: 1-212-854-5453

Website: www.goaskalice.columbia.edu

A MESSAGE TO TEENAGERS . . .
How to tell when drinking is becoming a problem

In order to help you determine whether or not you have a problem with alcohol, Alcoholics Anonymous has developed this simple 12-question quiz for teenagers. If you answer "yes" to one or more of these questions, you may want to take a closer look at how drinking may be affecting your life. The organizations listed in this chapter, as well as your parents and teachers, can be valuable sources of advice and help if you think you may have a drinking problem.

1. Do you drink because you have problems, or to relax?

2. Do you drink when you get mad at other people, like your parents or friends?

3. Do you prefer to drink alone, rather than with others?

4. Are your grades starting to slip? Are you goofing off on your job?

5. Did you ever try to stop drinking, and fail?

Hazelden Center for Youth and Families

A nonprofit treatment center that offers rehabilitation for youth and young adults suffering from chemical dependency. Website provides useful information and links to other resources.

Address: 11505 36th Avenue North, Plymouth, MN 55441-2398
Telephone: 1-800-257-7810
Website: www.hazelden.org

6. Have you begun to drink in the morning before school or work?

7. Do you gulp your drinks?

8. Do you ever experience memory loss due to your drinking?

9. Do you lie about your drinking?

10. Do you ever get into trouble when you're drinking?

11. Do you get drunk when you drink, even when you don't mean to?

12. Do you think it's cool to be able to hold your liquor?

The questions from the pamphlet "A Message to Teenagers" are reprinted with permission of Alcoholics Anonymous World Services, Inc. (A.A.W.S.). Permission to reprint does not mean that A.A.W.S. has reviewed or approved the contents of this book, or that A.A.W.S. necessarily agrees with the views expressed herein.

Mothers Against Drunk Driving (MADD)
Provides information on legislative actions and campaigns to eliminate drunk driving as well as efforts to curb underage drinking.
Address: P.O. Box 541688, Dallas, TX 7535401688
Telephone: 1-800-GET MADD (1-800-438-6233)
Website: www.madd.org

TEENS AND TREATMENT: The Straight Facts

The National Household Survey on Drug Abuse collects information on alcohol and drug use in the United States, as well as information that describes the individuals who seek treatment to stop or reduce alcohol or drug use. As the statistics suggest, alcohol-related problems don't discriminate on the basis of age, gender, or race—young men and women of all races sought treatment in 2000. Additionally, more people sought treatment for alcohol-related problems than for any illicit drug, and self-help groups, like the groups listed in this chapter, were the most common sources of treatment:

Age

- An estimated 0.2 million youths aged 12 to 17 received treatment for an alcohol problem (1.0 percent of all youths aged 12 to 17), and 0.4 million young adults aged 18 to 25 received treatment for an alcohol problem (1.4 percent of all adults aged 18 to 25).

Gender

- Among persons aged 12 or older, males were more than twice as likely as females to receive alcohol treatment in 2000 (1.4 vs. 0.5 percent, respectively). However, among youths aged 12 to 17, the percentage of males receiving treatment for an alcohol problem was not significantly higher than the percentage of females receiving treatment for an alcohol problem (1.1 vs. 0.9 percent, respectively).

National Association for Children of Alcoholics (NACOA)
Provides resources and information to children and families affected
by alcoholism.
Address: 11426 Rockville Pike, Suite 100, Rockville, MD 20852
Telephone: 1-888-55-4COAS (1-888-554-2627)
Website: www.nacoa.org

Race

- Among persons aged 12 or older, the rate for alcohol or illicit drug treatment during the 12 months prior to the interview was highest among American Indians/Alaska Natives (4.0 percent). However, this rate was not significantly different from the rate for whites (1.3 percent). The rate for African Americans was 1.5 percent, and the rate for Hispanics was 1.1 percent. Among Asians, 0.3 percent had received treatment for substance use problems in the past 12 months.

Frequency and Type of Treatment

- In 2000, among persons aged 12 or older, more people received treatment for alcohol at their most recent treatment in the past year than any other substance (1.9 million persons). This represents 68.0 percent of all people receiving treatment for a substance use problem in the past year.

- Among the 2.1 million persons aged 12 or older who received alcohol treatment in the past year, more people received treatment at a self-help group than any other location (0.5 million people). An estimated 0.3 million people received alcohol treatment at each of the following three locations: (a) an inpatient rehabilitation facility, (b) an outpatient rehabilitation facility, and (c) an outpatient mental health center.

Source: 2000 National Household Survey on Drug Abuse

National Council on Alcoholism and Drug Dependence, Inc (NCADD)

Provides information and education on alcoholism and other drug-related illnesses and addictions.

Address: 20 Exchange Place, Suite 2902, New York, NY 10005
Telephone: 1-800-NCA-CALL (1-800-622-2255)
Website: www.ncadd.org

National Highway Traffic Safety Administration

Provides statistics and information on traffic and automobile safety, including alcohol-related accidents and violations, from the U.S. Department of Transportation.

Address: 400 7th Street SW, Washington, D.C. 20590
Telephone: 1-888-DASH 2 DOT (1-888-327-4236)
Website: www.nhtsa.gov

National Institute on Alcohol Abuse and Alcoholism (NIAAA)

A division of the federal government's National Institutes of Health that provides summaries of alcohol-related topics, reviews of alcohol research, and a database of statistics on alcohol use and problems.

Address: 6000 Executive Blvd, Willco Building, Bethesda,
     MD 20892-7003
Telephone: 1-800-729-6688
Website: www.niaaa.nih.gov

Students Against Destructive Decisions (SADD)

A school-based youth organization that promotes teen empowerment and uses peer influence to spread the message of positive decision-making about things like underage drinking, drug use, and violence. SADD has local chapters in middle schools and high schools around the country.

Telephone: 1-877-SADD-INC (1-877-723-3462)
Website: www.saddonline.com

Substance Abuse and Mental Health Services Administration

Federal government office that provides information on substance abuse, including alcohol and other drug-related issues.

Address: P.O. Box 2345, Rockville, MD 20847-2345
Telephone: 1-310-443-0365
Website: www.samhsa.gov

Appendix

A Comparison of Teen Alcohol Use in Europe with Teen Alcohol Use in the United States

In 1999, sociologists at the Swedish Council for Information on Alcohol and other Drugs conducted school surveys of the tobacco, alcohol and illicit drug use of 95,000 10th grade students in 30 participating European countries. This survey, called the *European School Survey Project on Alcohol and Drugs (ESPAD)*, was specifically developed to be comparable to the Monitoring the Future (MTF) study in the United States. The results of the ESPAD and MTF surveys are very valuable to researchers in the United States and Europe, who rarely have the opportunity to compare substance abuse figures between countries. Let's review the results and compare the rates of alcohol and other drug use among teens in Europe with those in the United States:

Alcohol use in past 30 days. The MTF study finds that 40% of 10th grade students in the United States had consumed alcohol in the past 30 days. The ESPAD survey finds that an average of 61% of 10th grade students in the 30 participating European countries had consumed alcohol in the past 30 days (62% in Northern Europe, 63% in Southern Europe and 58% in Eastern Europe). This proportion varies among European countries from 36% in the former Yugoslav Republic of Macedonia (FYROM) to 85% in Denmark. FYROM was the only European country that had a lower rate than the United States.

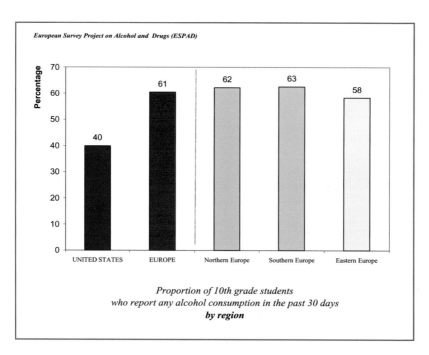

Proportion of 10th grade students
who report any alcohol consumption in the past 30 days
by region

There are two important concepts to consider when comparing the different rates of alcohol consumption between teens in European countries and teens in the United States. This first is *set*. Set is a person's expectation for the type of effect he or she will experience after using alcohol. This expectation is created by a person's total past experience—all that he or she has ever heard, read, seen, or thought about in reference to drinking. The second concept is *setting*. Setting is a person's physical, social, and cultural environment—the who, what, where, and when of the drinking experience.

The possible sociological and cultural differences suggested by these varying rates of alcohol consumption among teens in different countries may provide some insight into your own decision to drink. As mentioned in the first chapter of this book, alcohol is used regularly as part of the family meal in some cultures, which may account for the higher rates of alcohol in European countries where this practice is more common than in the United States. Would you be drinking with the same expectations (set) and setting (cultural environment), or is your drinking more likely to take place in secret or with friends at a party where there are no parents around?

Even if teens in Europe are drinking in "culturally acceptable" ways, however, it is a myth that more liberal drinking age laws and attitudes in Europe foster more responsible styles of drinking by teens. According to the MTF and ESPAD studies, there is no evidence that stricter drinking laws for teens in the United States is associated with a greater level of problematic drinking. Also, there is no evidence that the more liberal policies and drinking socialization practices in Europe are associated with lower levels of problematic drinking. In fact, according to the ESPAD and MTF survey comparisons:

- A greater percentage of European teens (compared to U.S. teens) report having five or more drinks in a row.

- About half of the European countries in the survey had higher prevalence rates for self-reported intoxication than the United States, about a quarter had lower rates, and about a quarter had rates that were more or less the same as the United States.

These results seem to suggest that regardless of the set or setting of alcohol consumption among teens, there will always be problematic drinking patterns.

Bibliography

Alters, Sandra. *Alcohol and Tobacco: America's Drugs of Choice.* Detroit, MI: Gale Group, Inc, 2002.

Barbour, Scott, ed. *Alcohol: Opposing Viewpoints.* San Diego, CA: Greenhaven Press, 1998.

Bennett, Linda A. and Ames, Genevieve M., eds. *The American Experience with Alcohol: Contrasting Cultural Perspectives.* New York: Plenum Press, 1985.

Braun, Stephen. *Buzz: The Science and Lore of Alcohol and Caffeine.* New York: Oxford University Press, 1996.

Epstein, J. F. *Substance Dependence, Abuse, and Treatment: Findings from the 2000 National Household Survey on Drug Abuse.* Rockville, MD: Substance Abuse and Mental Health Services Administration, Office of Aplied Studies, 2002.

FitzGerald, Kathleen Whalen. *Alcoholism: The Genetic Inheritance.* New York: Doubleday, 1988.

Glassner, Barry and Loughlin, Julia. *Drugs in Adolescent Worlds.* New York: St. Martin's Press, 1987.

Howard, George S. and Nathan, Peter E., eds. *Alcohol Use and Misuse by Young Adults.* Notre Dame, IN: University of Notre Dame Press, 1994.

Kinney, Jean and Leaton, Gwen. *Loosening the Grip: A Handbook of Alcohol Information,* 3rd ed. St. Louis, MO: Times/Mirror/Mosby College Publishing, 1987.

Lang, Alan R. *Alcohol: Teenage Drinking.* New York: Chelsea House Publishers, 1985.

National Institute on Drug Abuse. *Drug Abuse Prevention for the General Population.* Rockville, MD: U.S. Department of Health and Human Services, National Institutes of Health, 1997.

Office of Applied Studies. *Driving After Drug or Alcohol Use: Findings from the 1996 National Household Survey on Drug Abuse.* Rockville, MD: Department of Health and Human Services, Department of Transportation, 1998.

U.S. Department of Health and Human Services. *10th Special Report to the U.S. Congress on Alcohol and Health: Highlights from Current Research.* Rockville, MD: U.S. Department of Health and Human Services, National Institutes of Health, 2000.

Websites

American Council for Drug Education
www.Acde.org

Al-Anon/Alateen
www.Al-anon.alateen.org

Leadership to Keep Children Alcohol Free
www.Alcoholfreechildren.org/gs/stats/

Alcoholics Anonymous
www.Alcoholics-anonymous.org

Children of Alcoholics Foundation
www.Coaf.org

Indiana Prevention Resource Center
www.Drugs.indiana.edu

Hazeldon Foundation
www.Hazelden.org

PREVLINE
www.Health.org

KidsHealth
www.Kidshealth.org

National Association for Children of Alcoholics
www.Nacoa.org

National Institute on Alcohol Abuse and Alcoholism
www.Niaaa.nih.gov

National Library of Medicine
www.Nlm.nih.gov

PRIDE Surveys
www.Pridesurveys.com

Alcohol History Database
www.Scc.rutgers.edu/alcohol_history/

Science Daily
www.Sciencedaily.com

Further Reading

Books

Alters, Sandra. *Alcohol and Tobacco: America's Drugs of Choice.* Detroit, MI: Gale Group, Inc, 2002.

Black, Claudia. *Children of Alcoholics: Selected Readings.* Rockville, MD: National Association of Children of Alcoholics, 1995.

Brooks, Cathleen. *The Secret Everyone Knows.* Center City, MN: Hazelden Information, 1989.

Egendorf, Laura K., ed. *Teen Alcoholism.* San Diego, CA: Greenhaven Press, 2001.

Lang, Alan R. *Alcohol: Teenage Drinking.* New York: Chelsea House Publishers, 1985.

Leite, Evelyn. *Different Like Me: A Book for Teens Who Worry About Their Parent's Use of Alcohol/Drugs.* Minneapolis, MN: Johnson Institute Books, 1989.

McFarland, Rhoda. *Drugs and Your Parents.* Center City, MN: Hazelden Information, 1997.

Miner, Jane Claypool. *Alcohol and You.* London: Franklin Watts, Inc, 1997.

Mitchell, Haley R. *Teen Alcoholism.* Farmington Hills, MI: Lucent Books, 1997.

Ryerson, Eric. *When Your Parent Drinks Too Much: A Book for Teenagers.* New York: Facts on File, 1985.

Seixas, Judith. *Living with a Parent Who Drinks Too Much.* New York: William Morrow, 1983.

Torr, James D., ed. *Teens and Alcohol.* San Diego, CA: Greenhaven Press, 2001.

Websites

Alateen
www.Alateen.org

Children of Alcoholics Foundation
www.Coaf.org

Hazeldon Foundation
www.Hazelden.org

PREVLINE
www.Health.org

KidsHealth
www.Kidshealth.org

National Youth Anti-Drug Media Campaign
www.Mediacampaign.org/kidsteens/

National Association for Children of Alcoholics Foundation
www.Nacoa.org

Index

Picture Credits

About the Author

Heather Lehr Wagner is a writer and editor. She earned an M.A. from the College of William and Mary and a B.A. from Duke University. She has written several books for teens on global and family issues and is also the author of *Nicotine and Cocaine* in the DRUGS: THE STRAIGHT FACTS series. She lives with her husband and their three children in Pennsylvania.

About the Editor

David J. Triggle is a University Professor and a Distinguished Professor in the School of Pharmacy and Pharmaceutical Sciences at the State University of New York at Buffalo. He studied in the United Kingdom and earned his B.Sc. degree in Chemistry from the University of Southampton and a Ph.D. degree in Chemistry at the University of Hull. Following post-doctoral work at the University of Ottawa in Canada and the University of London in the United Kingdom, he assumed a position at the School of Pharmacy at Buffalo. He served as Chairman of the Department of Biochemical Pharmacology from 1971 to 1985 and as Dean of the School of Pharmacy from 1985 to 1995. From 1995 to 2001 he served as the Dean of the Graduate School, and as the University Provost from 2000 to 2001. He is the author of several books dealing with the chemical pharmacology of the autonomic nervous system and drug-receptor interactions, some four hundred scientific publications, and has delivered over one thousand lectures worldwide on his research.